**By David Grossman**

NOVELS

*The Smile of the Lamb*

*See Under: LOVE*

*The Book of Intimate Grammar*

*The Zigzag Kid*

*Be My Knife*

NONFICTION

*The Yellow Wind*

*Sleeping on a Wire*

# Death as a Way of Life

# DEATH AS A WAY OF LIFE

## Israel Ten Years After Oslo

David Grossman
Translated from the Hebrew by
Haim Watzman

Edited by Efrat Lev

Farrar, Straus and Giroux
New York

Farrar, Straus and Giroux
19 Union Square West, New York 10003


Distributed in Canada by Douglas & McIntyre Ltd.
Printed in the United States of America
First edition, 2003

Some of these essays and articles originally appeared in *al-Ayyam, The Guardian* (London), *Ha'aretz, Ma'ariv, The New York Times, Newsweek,* and *Yedioth Ahronoth.* "Seven Days: A Diary" first appeared in *Libération* (trans. Jean-Luc Allouche). "Suddenly, Human Contact" first appeared September 16, 1993, in the *Frankfurter Allgemeine Zeitung.* "The Holocaust Carrier Pigeon" first appeared in *Die Zeit.* The articles "Arafat Arrives in Gaza," "No Peace, No Security," "Beware, Opportunity Ahead," "The Pope's Visit to Israel," "Boy Killed in Gaza," "Hours Before the Elections," and "International Intervention, Please" first appeared in *La Repubblica.*



Library of Congress Cataloging-in-Publication Data
Grossman, David.
Death as a way of life : Israel ten years after Oslo / David Grossman ; translated from the Hebrew by Haim Watzman.— 1st ed.
p. cm.
ISBN 0-374-10211-2 (alk. paper)
1. Arab-Israeli conflict—1993—Peace. 2. Israel—Politics and government—1993– 3. Palestinian Arabs—Politics and government—1993– 4. Peace—Political aspects—Israel. 5. Fear—Political aspects—Israel. I. Title.

DS119.76.G77 2003
956.9405′4—dc21 2002044766

Designed by Debbie Glasserman

www.fsgbooks.com

10 9 8 7 6 5 4 3 2 1

# Contents

# Preface

Noise. That's the first word that comes into my mind when I think of the last ten years. So much noise. Gunshots and shouts, incendiary words and mournful laments, and explosions and demonstrations, and heaps of clichés and special broadcasts from the scenes of terrorist attacks, and calls for revenge and the throb of helicopters above and the screeching sirens of ambulances and the frantic rings of the telephone after each incident.

And within that whirlwind, in the eye of the storm, there is silence. It can't be heard; it is felt, in every cell of the body. A silence such as one feels in the brief moment between receiving bad news and comprehending it, between the blow and the pain.

This is the empty space in which every person, Israeli or Palestinian, knows with piercing certainty all that he does not want or does not dare to know. There, within himself, he understands—even if he denies it at the top of his lungs, with shouts, even gunshots—that his life is being dissipated, squandered in a pointless struggle, and that his identity and self-respect and the one life he has to live are being endlessly expropriated from him in a conflict that could have been resolved long ago.

It is too painful to admit. The thought is too intolerable.

And that's the source of the constant, overwhelming urge to flee that silence, to go back out into the familiar noise to which we have somehow—it's hard to remember just how—become accustomed. We actually don't function too badly there. They (that is, "the enemies") will not break us. Justice is on our side. There is no choice. We shall live by the sword and die by the sword.

But there, in that quiet place, the noise from outside is silenced. There, laid bare, stripped of any national, religious, tribal, or social garments that protect him, a man sits alone, curled up inside himself, like someone who has perpetrated a truly horrible deed, and who comes to understand the crime he has committed, that he continues to commit, outside the silence, against others and against himself.

Few of us, Israeli or Palestinian, can be proud of what we have done during these past years, of what we have collaborated in, whether actively or in passive acceptance of the noise—the collaboration of turning away our eyes, of suspending our souls, of anesthetizing ourselves.

This book contains a few dozen articles and responses to particularly turbulent moments in the years since the signing of the Oslo Accords in 1993. I am not a journalist—if I had my way, I would lock myself up at home and write only fiction. But the daily reality in which I live surpasses anything I could imagine, and it seeps into my deepest parts. Sometimes, writing an article is the only way for me to decipher, to understand, and to survive from day to day.

I also write articles because of the noise. Because I often feel suffocated, claustrophobic, caught between the deceptive, deceitful words that all interested parties—the government, the army, the media—are constantly trying to impose on us, their subjects, who must live in this disaster area. Sometimes, if we reformulate a situation that already seems beyond hope and set in stone, we are able to recall that there is in fact no divine decree that dooms us to be the helpless victims of apathy and paralysis.

I have to admit that many times I often feel that words can no longer penetrate the screen of horror. It is difficult to speak to another person's heart when, all around, human beings are being blown up and children are being torn to pieces. At such moments, I very much want, instead of writing, to run through the streets screaming.

Some opinions and hopes I expressed, some assessments I believed in, have been proved wrong after they were written. I include these writings in this collection because they, too, reflect, or so I think, the process that many of us have undergone. I include them here because I do not want to deny what I—and not just I—have experienced. Nor do I wish to refute my hopes and wishes.

Sometimes, when I take a look at the map and see the thing that is at issue, I grow despondent. Here is the minuscule state of Israel, whose size on the map isn't even large enough to contain its name and whose central waistline measures less than seven miles. It's surrounded by hostile countries and peoples, several of them drenched in a wave of fundamentalist Islamism, saturated with a hatred of Jews as Jews—explicitly declaring their desire to destroy the Jewish state. I feel, in my body, how dread and despair transform the fingers of an outstretched hand into a fist. It is not difficult to comprehend how, in this situation, the instinctive urge of Israelis is to raise their defenses even higher. It is easy to understand why they are tempted to follow aggressive, bellicose leaders; to hide inside a suit of armor, frightened, suspicious, and scarred by past memories, in expectation of the next collision.

What awaits us? Who is wise enough to know? I tend to believe that for the foreseeable future, our lives here will be made up of a continual series of confrontations, small and large. My hope is that, gradually, the fuses of the conflict will be neutralized, that weariness will overcome both sides, and that painful acceptance of truth will force Israelis and Palestinians to turn to nonviolent means of achieving their goals.

But even if we are doomed to years of violence and animosity, to fragile peace agreements that will be violated over and over again, we must keep creating an alternative. We must reiterate the possibility, denied and repudiated today, of peaceful coexistence. Our two peoples must strengthen among themselves, and among the members of the other nation, those who are truly interested in peace, those who are already prepared for painful compromise. If we don't do this, the entire arena will be wide open for the extremists, the violent, and the warmongers. If we don't do this, our children will remember only dimly what is really worth fighting for, what they can aspire to. It is frightening to see how easy it is to forget that. How quickly the dearest, most important things grow indistinct and are swallowed up by the noise. This, perhaps, is the most depressing discovery of the last two years—the heady attraction of hatred, of the hunger for revenge. In a single breath, it is as if a veneer of culture and humanity has been removed from the two peoples to reveal brutishness and barbarity. Sometimes, viewing the atrocities that these two peoples inflict on each other, a person loses not only his desire to live in this region, but his desire to live at all.

The chance of extricating ourselves from these inner snares thus depends not a little on the ability to resist the way of thinking expressed by the phrases "There is no choice" and "There is no partner." In this struggle, the battle lines today are drawn not between Israelis and Palestinians, but rather between those who are unwilling to come to terms with despair and those who wish to turn it into a way of life.

That struggle is at the heart of this book—thirty-four articles; one story, still being written.

David Grossman
Jerusalem, December 2002

# Death as a Way of Life

## Suddenly, Human Contact

SEPTEMBER 1993

*Following secret negotiations in Norway, Israeli prime minister Yitzhak Rabin and PLO leader Yasir Arafat signed, in the White House on September 13, 1993, a Declaration of Principles—known as the Oslo Accords. The sides "agree that it is time to put an end to decades of confrontation and conflict, recognize their mutual legitimate and political rights, and strive to live in peaceful coexistence and mutual dignity and security, and achieve a just, lasting and comprehensive peace settlement and historic reconciliation through the agreed political process." The Oslo Accords provided only a framework for a solution rather than a final determination of all conditions of peace, including borders and relations between the two peoples.*

I

"And now," the newscaster chortled, "they're shaking hands!" And then he added, in a hushed and astonished whisper, "They're simply—shaking hands."

Through nearly one hundred years of conflict, the two peoples have been in physical contact untold times, especially during the last sixty years. There have been thousands of moments in which body brushed body. For the most part, these have been violent encounters. The aspirations, anger, and distress of one people drained suddenly into the blade of a knife, or crystallized into a flying rock. And the aspirations of the other people, with their anger and fears, would transmogrify into lead bullets, clubs, police handcuffs, and soldiers.

On the face of it, the contact in the ceremony on the White House lawn was really the contact of two symbols. For many of his countrymen, Yitzhak Rabin is the prototypical Israeli. He symbolizes, almost stereotypically, the Sabra, the new Israeli Jew. He's native-born, fought in the War of Independence, rose to the rank of chief of staff, and led the army to its great victory in the Six-Day War. He's the salt of the land of Israel.

To the Palestinians, Rabin symbolizes the evil of the Israeli occupation. They cannot forget his order at the beginning of the Intifada to "break their bones." They see him as the essence of Israeli militarism, cruelty, and callousness to their suffering.

Arafat, to many Israelis, is the ultimate enemy. To them he's crafty, slippery, and can't be trusted. If you turn your back on him, they fear, he'll stab you. For thirty years, Israel's leaders have taught their people to view Arafat as a two-legged beast, Hitler's heir, a creature not fit for human society, who under no circumstances can be a partner in a dialogue.

But most Palestinians see Arafat as a symbol of the Palestinian life force. He represents survival in the face of hardship and persecution. For them, Arafat is the oppressed and wretched refugee who finally—thanks to his patience, courage, and determination—will win what he has demanded from his powerful and heartless enemy.

Two symbols shook hands, and the contact suddenly became human. It is a kind of contact consisting of reluctance and revulsion, as well as instinctive curiosity, and even a smile. Contact between two flesh-and-blood human beings.

The two made painful concessions in the Declaration of

Principles. On each side there are individuals who oppose the agreement and who see it as a defeat for their leader. But none of the opponents—not among us and not among the Palestinians—can offer an alternative course of action that has any real value.

Rabin knows deep in his heart that he has, with his own hands, established the Palestinian state he has so feared. Arafat understands that he has given up his dream of establishing a greater Palestine that would include the territory on which Israel stands. Israel will have to accept armed Palestinian police forces, the Palestinians an Israeli military presence on the border between Israel and Jordan. Israel has made an immediate and concrete concession of territories and security assets. The Palestinians have, for the time being, conceded mostly aspirations and dreams. Yet I do not really know which side has made the more painful concession.

## II

For many long years the Palestinians stood outside history. They lived within larger-than-life mythical memories of the past and aspirations for a heroic future. Like children embroidering fantasies of comfort and revenge out of the threads of their pain, they sought to flee the oppressive and humiliating present. In such unrealism, such conditions of weightlessness, hopes become entirely disconnected from the possible. For years the Palestinians cultivated illusions and believed in them. It has been embarrassing and galling to read the Palestinian National Covenant, its definition of the "Palestinian identity," the statement of the Palestinian state's goals, and to compare them to reality and to the geopolitical balance of power in the region.

The agreement made with the Palestinians will bring them back to history. If a people receive a place of their own, they can also return to time, to the natural progress of history. With such a people, one can begin to conduct negotiations between equals and to establish tolerable neighborly relations.

I don't wish for anything more than that, but also not for anything less. Unlike many Israelis—including many on the left—I do not seek a "let's make up and never see each other again" kind of peace, or a high and impenetrable wall between Israel and Palestine.

I believe that the best thing for the two peoples is to maintain as many connections of different kinds as possible. Economic, commercial, cultural, touristic, and athletic ties, in order to peg the new tent we've erected to the ground of reality with thousands of ropes and tent pins.

We should keep in mind that these are two industrious, ambitious nations, quick to adjust to new situations. Although we have ignored and dismissed each other as nations for many years, on the individual level it has been possible to sense that we have here two people with a natural ability to talk with each other. There are similarities of character and temperament, even sense of humor.

I should stress that I am not speaking of love between the nations. There is no place here for idealization. Not for the Palestine Liberation Organization, which has committed especially repulsive acts in its years of struggle (one entry requirement has been proof that the candidate has murdered a Jewish child and abused the body), and certainly not for the Palestinians as a people, whose culture, values, and very being have been worn down by decades of oppression by the Turks, the Jordanians, and the Israelis. It is not only power that corrupts. Weakness can be no less corrupting. Even the Intifada, which began as a heroic initiative of a nation seeking liberty, became in the space of only two years a welter of mutual killings, a rebellion run by religious extremists and common criminals. Yet despite it all, we would not have reached the current agreement without the Intifada.

I can certainly understand that the Palestinians loathe Israel, which to them looks like a militaristic, cruel, oppressive state. Despite Israel's attempt to conduct an "enlightened occupation" (a conceit at best—no such thing is possible), the behavior of the Israeli Defense Forces during twenty-six years of occupation has left major scars in the Palestinian collective memory. The state of occupation has been debilitating for Israeli democracy and for the rule of law. Violence has permeated our lives. I don't know how many years will pass before children on both sides cease being afflicted at birth with hatred.

But who can hope for love between nations? Who really loves anyone in this world? (Of course, I'm referring not to people but to nations.) Do the English love the French? Do the Germans love the Russians? Perhaps we should even ask: Do the West Germans and East Germans love each other?

"Interests" is the key word, and it is the guarantee that the agreement will work. The two peoples have signed on to the agreement because they understand that they have no other choice. After decades of mutual bloodletting, they have come to terms with the idea that if they do not live side by side they will perish together, in a maelstrom that will engulf the entire region. It is existential interest that pushed these two reluctant peoples into each other's arms. The United States and Japan, and the Europeans led by Germany, now have to turn peace into a practical and enticing option for both sides. A flourishing economy, new jobs, a sense of freedom, reinforcement of everything in life that was damaged or paralyzed during the years of occupation and Intifada—all these can significantly strengthen those Palestinians who want peace. Similarly, the right-wing extremists in Israel will have difficulty arguing with a concrete improvement in the economy, in the quality of life, in the sense of security. The fundamentalists of Hamas will fight a war of despair and no quarter. They will try to create a nightmare atmosphere. Only a robust creative reality, full of life and hope, will succeed in withstanding them. We need to begin creating that reality now, immediately.

Neither romantic love, then, nor a high wall. I dream of two countries separated by a distinct border. A border that will make clear to each state the space in which it exists as a political entity, as a national identity. If there's a border, there is an identity. There is a new living reality in which this identity can bleed out the poison of illusions and begin to heal.

One more important thing: This is a condition in which—years from now—the two sides will be able to give themselves a new kind of definition—not one contrasted with an enemy, but one that turns inward. One dependent not on the fear that they might be destroyed but instead on the natural development of a nation, on its system of values and the various facets of its character. This is a decisive change. For years, both sides have suspended the internal dialogue that each must have. The state of continual conflict was a reason and an excuse for not addressing their fundamental, authentic problems, a reason for just trying to survive one more violent conflagration. I can definitely see that such a new process of defining ourselves, the Israelis, will bring about tremors and changes. It will require a painful assessment of our definition of ourselves today in relation to our Jewish heritage. It will force us to confront our complicated history anew, and to consider the possibility of choosing a new way of relating to the world outside us.

If peace is established between us and all the Arab countries, we will also be able, finally, to internalize the fact that we are part of the Middle East. We will comprehend that our presence here is not the result of some bureaucratic-geographical error, but rather that this is the place in which our lives will henceforth be conducted, and it would be well for us to open ourselves to the world and to the culture of our neighbors. Clearly, such a step can be taken only if we have partners, if the Arab countries no longer view Israel as "a cancerous growth of imperialism" (as Israel has been termed on many an occasion in the Arab press) but rather as an integral, stimulating, and vital part of the Middle East.

If we can reach and live with this vision of the end of days, we Israelis may well permit ourselves—after years of instinctive self-denial—to believe that we have a future. That we may dare to believe that we will finally have continuity and prospects. That death will not cast its shadow on everything in our lives. Perhaps we will be able to free ourselves from that sense of doom that lies deep down in our collective consciousnesses—that, for us, life is only latent death.

This is the true meaning of self-determination. I have always believed that when Israel agrees to grant this right to the Palestinians, it will also win it for itself. Now the moment has come for the Israelis, for the Palestinians, and for the other sane nations in the region. Here it is now: the Future.

## Arafat Arrives in Gaza

JUNE 1994

*In accordance with the May 1994 Cairo Agreement on the Gaza Strip and the Jericho Area, Israeli forces withdrew from Jericho and most of the Gaza Strip. On July 1, 1994, Yasir Arafat returned to Gaza for the first time in thirty-three years. He crossed the border from Egypt and was welcomed by a large, cheering Palestinian crowd. The picture of Arafat, wearing his usual army uniform and kaffiyah and carrying a gun, flashing a victory sign, was a difficult sight for many Israelis. About one hundred thousand Israeli right-wing supporters demonstrated in Jerusalem, calling for death to Rabin and to Arafat.*

Arafat arrives in Gaza, and half the Israeli nation jumps up shouting, "It's defeat, the beginning of the end of the Jewish state, what will become of us, how humiliating!"

Indeed, in the "old order," the equation was clear—if one side gains, the other side loses. Every gain comes at the other's expense. But since the Yom Kippur War of 1973, this perception of reality has been called into question. We won the war with the Egyptians, but the Egyptians didn't lose. In the peace negotiations, the Egyptians ostensibly won by receiving the entire Sinai Peninsula. But we didn't lose, because we created a state of peace and began the very long process of being accepted in the Middle East.

The Palestinians began an Intifada in 1987 and won, because they forced us to realize what we were doing to them, but the truth is that we did not lose, because, finally, the Intifada opened the way for us to save ourselves from what the occupation had done to us.

The same is true today. Arafat arrived in Gaza. The Palestinians in the territories will surely be drunk with joy. One can presume that their very happiness will irk many of us. One may also presume that the television cameras will do their best to bring into our homes Palestinians who get carried away by euphoria and say precisely those things that all of us fear, giving voice to their subliminal hope to return to Jaffa and Haifa. There will also be expressions of contempt for Israel, and there will be many Israelis who will feel the humiliation of defeat.

But the victory of the Palestinians is not our defeat. They have made a great gain, for which they have fought and paid a great price. They are beginning to make real a dream of many years. But thanks to the new consciousness that arose in September 1993—which will expunge the dichotomy of "either us or them"—we Israelis can also feel a sense of achievement today. Because today it is us *and* them.

The tragedy is that both "us" and "them" come into this new partnership scarred and wounded, crippled in body and soul. All of us, Israelis and Palestinians, are the children of this conflict, which has bequeathed us all the deformities of hatred and violence. Both sides require almost superhuman strength to break out of the spiral of murder and reprisal. As a result, it is sometimes difficult to remember what our basic interest is, and to take joy in their joy, and wish them, for our own sakes, success. May they overcome all those among them who seek to turn the wheel back, those who have become so accustomed to the deformities war has imposed on them that they refuse, with all their might, to be healed of them. They even try to persuade others not to undergo the surgery that, while painful, will heal them in the end.

Despite all this, Arafat will come to Gaza, and we may also permit ourselves to feel admiration for the climax of the struggle conducted by this man and the entire Palestinian people. The fact that it has been directed against us need not blind us. A struggle for independence, self-sacrifice, and courage are values we were educated in, and in which we educate our children. Some of the methods the Palestinians used in their struggle were despicable and cruel, but the acts we committed against them do not give us a standing to preach to them. There was a war, and we still feel its convulsions, but now some sort of doorway to peace has opened, and one part of our growing pains in this new situation is the need to acknowledge our rival's courage and determination. The Palestinian people, so derided, so mistreated during the last hundred years, are today standing before their first-ever chance for a life of honor and independence. Instead of hysterical demonstrations by Israelis who are too cowardly for peace, we should today be offering generosity, to ourselves as well, and we should understand that, together, we have made another important step ahead. Together—the two of us—we have won something that is much greater than either the Palestinians or the Israelis alone.

# The Holocaust Carrier Pigeon

JANUARY 1995

*This article was written specifically for German readers and was published in the German newspaper* Die Zeit *in commemoration of the fiftieth anniversary of the liberation of Auschwitz by the Soviet Army, on January 27, 1945.*

## I

It has been reported here that Germany is hoping that the ceremonies marking the fiftieth anniversary of the liberation of the death camps will also symbolize a historic reconciliation between the German and Jewish peoples. Holocaust survivors in Israel were outraged and protested. The approach of this significant date has again raised, with great intensity, questions about the relations between the two peoples, and about the need for, and the possibility of, reconciliation.

It's not easy for me to address the German reader about the Holocaust. I almost always feel as if I am not saying exactly what I intend to say. There's always some slight distortion, either of excess caution or of the opposite, overstatement. Sometimes, instead of expressing my own private pain, I find myself speaking as a representative. Or I address the person facing me as a spokesman. The relationships are complex, so both sides are often tempted—consciously or not—to become manipulative. For myself, I am aware to what extent insult is the dominant sentiment within me when I think about the Holocaust. Not wrath and not hatred or a desire for revenge; I am rather bitterly insulted by the fact that human beings were treated this way. I know that there is nothing like insult to trap me in puerile, helpless resentment, humiliating in itself.

On the other hand, I sometimes meet Germans who are so strangely and enthusiastically addicted to overwhelming, total feelings of guilt that any practical dialogue with them is impossible. This guilt may also make dialogue among themselves impossible. I'm similarly disgusted, incidentally, by the manner in which certain Israelis behave in their encounters with Germans. It's as if they are declaring: "We will never withdraw from the territory we have conquered in the German conscience." Both these approaches are unacceptable. But is there another way? Is it already possible, fifty years later, to find the right voice, a clean voice, for discussion?

## II

I have frequently been invited to meetings between Israeli and German intellectuals. Twice I accepted the invitations. I used to believe that *both* sides had to bear the burden of what happened in the Holocaust. In a twisted way, I regarded both, the Germans and the Jews, as "partners" in a terrifying historic event, and it seemed that in order to loosen the ties suffocating the souls of both nations, we now needed each other.

I no longer believe this. True, we must talk. Talking is useful even to remind ourselves of what is sometimes in doubt—that it is still possible to believe in humankind. But I feel that, to be prepared for real dialogue, each of the two parties must first learn to speak with itself. To utterly cleanse the "story it tells itself" of any idealization and demonization, and to be very much on guard against manipulation. Perhaps, to reach such clarity, both nations need to heal completely—not only from the consequences of the Holocaust, but also from the abnormality of each of their cultures and histories, which allowed the Holocaust to take place in the way that it did.

It seems to me that Israelis are now, more than in the past, able to conduct this dialogue among themselves, even if we are still at the beginning of the road. Israelis have, in recent years, done much to address painful questions. These include the arrogant insensitivity that caused Israelis to blame the Holocaust's victims for having gone to their deaths "like lambs to the slaughter," without defending themselves. There's also the cruelty with which native Israelis treated the survivors in the first years of the new state—demanding that they remain silent, that they hide themselves from public attention, that they feel shame for what they endured and even for having survived.

But there are other, more challenging questions that still haven't been touched. How did the Jewish people—as a nation and as a society—find itself trapped in a situation that allowed the extermination of a third of its population? This happened despite the fact that between 1917 and 1933 the Jews had the alternative of building themselves a national life and a political entity in Palestine. Why did the nation not have the power to save itself from the warped circumstances of the Diaspora before anti-Semitism reached its most extreme form in the Holocaust? And how can we free ourselves today from the tragic deformation that the Holocaust still dictates in so many areas of life and of consciousness? This is evident in our absolute, almost eerie insecurity about whether our children and we have a future, and in our feeling that death still shadows us, so that we are doomed to experience life as a living death.

There are other questions as well. How can we purge ourselves of our self-victimization, yet also adopt the right attitude toward the great power we have today, and toward our aggressive and cruel urges? How can we cope with our problematic perception of ourselves as a "chosen people," when chosenness always contains an element of exclusion or even of a curse? How can a nation that perceives itself as unique and special learn to live with the trivialities of daily life, a life devoid of miracles and catastrophes? How can it finally find the right place for itself in the family of nations?

We won't get the answers to these most piercing questions from the Germans. They aren't equipped to respond to them. But can we, Israeli Jews, respond to the fundamental questions that the Holocaust and World War II raised among the Germans?

III

Sometimes I wonder why the Germans so desperately need the presence of an Israeli at their discussions of World War II and the Holocaust. Is it that those who want to have such discussions, yet are anxious about them, need such a presence to jump-start the process? Perhaps some unconsciously seek absolution from the Jewish representatives, an absolution that no person is permitted to ask for and no person empowered to grant? Just as in modern Jewish discourse about the Holocaust, the Germans must do the major part of the work within themselves. The fundamental questions that World War II and the Holocaust raise have no necessary connection to Jews or Israelis. The German discourse on the Holocaust is, first and foremost, an internal German one. It touches on questions of identity and memory and education, and of the still complicated attitude toward the concept of homeland (*Heimat*). There is also the question of anti-Semitic concepts in German culture and thought, of attitudes to force and militarism. These latter are especially pressing as Germany becomes the strongest power in Europe and with nothing to brake it except its own self-restraint. And, of course, there is also the question of Germany's willingness and readiness to adopt democracy in its most profound way, granting legitimacy to other entities and desires.

A small linguistic matter catches my attention whenever I visit Europe, especially German-speaking countries. People often talk to me about "what happened *then*." "Then"—that is, once, in the past, things happened, but they no longer do, it's all over. But in Hebrew, or in Yiddish (actually, in any language that Jews use to talk about the Holocaust), people never speak of "then." They speak of "there." "There" indicates that in that "there"—not only in Germany, but in the range of human behavior—the thing still exists. Or happens. And in any case, it's not over. Certainly not for us.

Because we Israelis have almost no choice. It's becoming clearer to us: as time passes and it is possible to approach the facts, ever more powerful tidal waves of memories and emotions flood Israeli consciousness. Only two months ago, a television program about the attempt made during the war to ransom Jews from the Nazis captivated the entire country. Dozens of broadcast hours and numerous newspaper articles were devoted to the effort. With a single touch on the button of memory, the entire Holocaust broke forth within us with a force that caught us by surprise. We again realized that the new generation, the so-called new Israelis—supposedly fearless, devoid of their parents' anxieties—find themselves constantly confronting the memory of the Holocaust. They are doomed to revisit it on all levels of life, in their mental associations, in their moral choices, in their behavioral codes. Time and again, we discover that even if we reject the role, almost each one of us is a carrier pigeon for the Holocaust.

Israel does not always treat the Holocaust appropriately. Sometimes we manipulate ourselves. We turn those anxieties into a worldview and system of values. We idealize the victims, whom we often refer to as the "Holocaust martyrs." Among our youth, we create a one-dimensional identification between Jewish experience in the Holocaust and the overall meaning of being Jewish. Tens of thousands of high school students, on the verge of their enlistment in the army, make pilgrimages to Auschwitz to discover their "roots." For nonreligious young Jews, the Holocaust often becomes the central element in their national identity, taking up a bit of the space filled in others by religious identity. All these distortions still exist, but today's children at least do not have to grow up with the same taboos that my generation had. That suffocating silence, from which terrifying whispers sometimes escaped, the screams of our parents' nightmares, the rumors that our imagination could not comprehend—all were part of our lives.

## IV

Israelis have no choice but to confront the Holocaust each day. I think it's easier for Germans to ignore it. A young German can *choose* to take an interest, to purposely address the question of his parents' actions. On the face of it, one can understand the natural desire many Germans have to rid themselves of the burden of "the bad times" and of the sense that all Germans will forever have to pay the price of their parents' crimes. Perhaps this is the source of the somewhat embarrassing haste with which certain German politicians seek a kind of "instant reconciliation."

But the burden that became unbearable during that war cannot be quickly set aside, and will certainly not disappear as a result of silence and by being ignored. It requires a very long process of identity construction and education. Today's neo-Nazis demonstrate, in their dynamism and their drawing power, that the burden is still palpable. The German regime's (ambivalent?) tolerance of the neo-Nazis gives the impression that, in many ways, Germany is still only at the very beginning of a real discussion of its character.

I'm trying to write in a measured and rational way, but I feel how my emotions are suddenly surging. I want to talk about the simple, concrete things that still hurt me, fifty years later. There are the Holocaust survivors who, during the Gulf War, dispersed their families to different parts of Israel "so that at least someone will survive." I myself was only able, only brave enough to visit Germany after my name had appeared on a book cover—believing that this way no one could kill me anonymously, as a number, because now I had a first and last name in Germany. I want to write about the wild, primal fear that overcame me when the two Germanys united and I was lying in my bed in a hotel in Mainz, listening to the cheering crowds. I need to ponder over that split second of hesitation and awkwardness I hear in the voices of Germans when they say the word "Jew," as if the word is still prohibited. There's also the walk I always take when I visit Munich, through the beautiful Englischer Garten. I never walk there alone. I always take companions with me—Walter Benjamin, Kurt Tucholsky, Else Lasker-Schüler, Ernst Lubitsch, Franz Werfel, Alfred Döblin, Nelly Sachs, people who were once in Munich and others who never were. On these walks I always take a book written by one of them, or a memory of a poem they wrote or a film they made. We walk together and talk, and I constantly wonder, What is it like to feel like a hunted animal in the midst of all this beauty?

There are so many things to say, but I feel that in another moment I might fall into the insult trap that I mentioned before, so I must be careful. Fifty years is too short a period for the wound to heal. It's too early to sum up, and there's no urgent need to speak about reconciliation. After all, there is no feud between Israelis and Germans today. On the contrary, there are widespread ties in almost every area, a growing closeness and mutual curiosity. But at the tragic points of contact, the wound is still gaping. No person has the moral authority to cover it with a false bandage of ceremonies and declarations. No person has a right to decide on the date on which the scab begins to form, when the responsibility reaches its expiration date. We still have a long way to go.

## Yes, Prime Minister

APRIL 1995

*After the signing of the Oslo Accords in 1993, negotiations between Israel and the Palestinians moved on two separate tracks, one toward interim Palestinian self-government and another toward a permanent settlement. The interim track culminated with the Israeli-Palestinian Interim Agreement on the West Bank and the Gaza Strip, known as Oslo II, which Israeli prime minister Yitzhak Rabin and PLO chairman Yasir Arafat signed on September 28, 1995. This agreement divided the West Bank and Gaza into three zones, each with distinct borders and rules for administrative and security controls. Area A, including nearly all the Gaza Strip and six West Bank cities, was to be under exclusive Palestinian control; Area B was to include 450 Palestinian towns and villages in the West Bank, where the Palestinians would have civilian control and Israel would retain responsibility for security; Area C was to include mostly unpopulated areas of the West Bank and would be controlled exclusively by Israel.*

During a meeting last week with Palestinian intellectuals, an Israeli asked, "You, our Palestinian colleagues, know just as well as we do that the current difficult spot in the peace process is only a passing moment, and that in the end, after extended negotiations, you will receive what you want—a sovereign Palestinian state and separation of the two nations from each other. Why, then, don't we hear more of your voices within your society? Why don't you say this to your compatriots? It's precisely you who are supposed to be the farsighted vanguard, which can point out the advantages and hopes that the process offers. Why are you, of all people, silent?"

"Because we ourselves no longer believe very much in the process, as we once did" was the reply. "Because we look around us each day and see that large-scale land expropriations still continue, that roads are being paved around each city and village, that the settlements are being enlarged through massive construction projects. We are beginning to feel that, once again, just as in every contact we've had with the Israelis, you will mislead us, that you will defeat us; only this time it will happen in such a devious and oppressive way that we will have no chance at all of recovering from it."

This dialogue will not reveal anything new to people who are in contact with the Palestinians. But it may well be that most of the Israeli public, especially that part of it which supports the peace process, is not sufficiently aware of these sentiments. This response from our Palestinian colleagues, all of whom support peace with Israel and have paid a heavy personal price as a result, requires the members of the Israeli peace camp to make an honest assessment of the (horrific) possibility that we are deluding ourselves.

It is astonishing that this question is not being asked in the moderate, liberal left, how it is repressed and avoided. For decades the left has been exerting a huge effort—acting, thinking, framing ideas, organizing on a large scale. It has succeeded in creating a public atmosphere that, at a fortuitous moment—thanks to the Palestinian uprising—seeped into the reluctant minds of our politicians and propelled them into negotiations.

But ever since the Oslo agreement, this same left has been afflicted with almost complete paralysis. The usual excuse is, of course, that now the government is carrying out what the left predicted and desired and fought for. But is this statement still valid? Is the plan, as it looks today, really what the left had in mind? Have the negotiations with the Palestinians really been conducted in a way that we think will bring about normal neighborly relations, or are they turning (perhaps intentionally?) into one more stage of humiliation for the Palestinians, into an imposition of surrender on them? Is the peace process in fact ensuring that war will continue?

How can it be that in recent months almost no clear voices have been raised on the left asking these questions? Can it be that we on the left are censoring ourselves, preventing this question from even being asked (with all good intention, so that we do not interfere with the process)? Perhaps, in our silence, we are collaborating with a historic debacle whose bitter fruits Israel will have to digest for generations. How can it be that the Peace Now movement isn't sending out thousands of volunteers to intersections each day to make this other voice heard? Why isn't it organizing mass demonstrations, precisely now, to exert pressure in the direction where it has always tried to lead? What has happened to the movement? What has happened to the government ministers from the pro-peace Meretz Party?

After all, huge pressure is being exerted on Yitzhak Rabin from the other direction, and its results can be seen in the street, in the public opinion surveys, and soon at the polls (its effect on Mr. Rabin's political and personal behavior is especially notable). Yet on the left—silence. True, the far-left Gush Shalom movement is asking such questions, but they are getting no response and no attention from the more moderate, and larger, part of the left. "How suddenly feeble you are, how have you ceased to give aid," the poet Chaim Nachman Bialik chided the Zionist leadership in his 1931 poem "You Have Seen the Shortness of Your Reach." Those lines are now addressed to us: as if we, the people of the word, of the book, of thought, become ineffectual when ideas turn to reality. As if we thought that from here on out, peace is the job of the doers rather than the thinkers. A kind of supernatural sense of security has overtaken us since Oslo, a strange certainty that may well be based on nothing more than a naïve wishful hope that we have placed our pledge in the hands of a trustworthy emissary who will bring it to its destination, and that from the point forward, peace will prevail.

It is today, of all times, that a voice must come from the left, a voice with great force to pressure the government. The left has a unique talent for blazing a trail out of entrapment and immobility, away from petty squabbles with the Palestinians. There is no good reason to leave the field to the politicians. Especially not now. If we abandon it to them, we will truly be worthy of the dismissive term "bleeding hearts."

The bitter truth is that most of those who are today "leading" the process were not willing to enter into it until it was more or less forced upon them. Most of them did not read the map properly, did not discern the subterranean flow, the pressure building up with explosive force. After all, it was the long hesitation of the politicians of the right and the left, their denseness, their mental paralysis, their pandering to their voting public, that got us stuck in the disheartening situation we find ourselves in today. Why should we believe that all of a sudden, and in a much more delicate and complex situation, they would be able to reinvent themselves as more flexible and farsighted leaders? To what extent are they really able to change? Imagine a child who plays constantly with a puzzle made from a picture of a wolf. Suddenly the child is told to build, out of the same pieces, a picture of a *dove.* That, more or less, is the present dilemma of Prime Minister Rabin.

The question we need to ask is: When Rabin speaks (sincerely!) about wanting peace with the Palestinians, is he speaking of the most desirable, true peace for Israel in the long run, the peace for which the left has struggled all these years? The impression is growing stronger that what Mr. Rabin really means is an expanded security arrangement that will fence the Palestinians into autonomous areas of confinement, surrounded and separated one from the other by a dense network of Israeli roads, roadblocks, and settlements.

The distance that Prime Minister Rabin has traveled up until now is worthy of admiration. Few leaders in the world or in Israel have the ability to do what he has done. Still, it is difficult to avoid the impression that the belief in the use of force and the fighting instinct that are inherent in his character (an instinct that was most vital in other situations and times) are now preventing him from going the full distance. And this road has to be walked to its end. There's no stopping before the destination is reached. If we don't walk to the end, we will find ourselves walking back the way we came.

When it comes down to it, the peace process is, despite reports to the contrary, reversible. Many situations and procedures that were much more solid than this limping peace process were considered "irreversible," their disappearance "impossible," until they suddenly came to an end, and from then on the situation arranged itself in a different way around them. If Arafat becomes inactive, naturally or through a violent act; if Rabin continues to hesitate and to contend with Arafat instead of understanding that their fates are intertwined; if the Likud wins the elections; if the peace process is suspended for a few weeks after each major terrorist attack—if only one of these events happens (or any one of a myriad of others), there will be no peace. Not with the Palestinians or, as a result, with the Syrians. The entire regional movement toward peace, problematic as it may be, will be frozen. But it won't be cold here—within a short time Syria will begin to give us hell in Lebanon. The Intifada will renew itself in the strangled, despairing "territories," this time with violence we have not yet seen.

In order to change this scenario fundamentally, we need to make a much more daring move. We need to shake off the repudiating, ungenerous, derisory attitude our representatives have taken toward the Palestinians during the negotiations. There's no question that our position in the negotiations is much more comfortable—we have the "merchandise" and they need it; we are strong and they are weak. Error: it's not at all clear that we are only giving and they are only taking. Neither is it obvious that they need this peace more than we do. If that were really the case, Israel would not have been so quick to enter the process.

Isn't it too late? When will we begin to hear voices that are at least as determined and aggressive as those on the right, demanding of Rabin that he not "defeat them" all that much? That we be much more generous, that we rise above our instinct to wrangle with them, that we remain committed to our original intentions? Or might it be that, deep in their hearts, those on the liberal left also want, even just a bit, to defeat the Palestinians and so "prove"—what?—the left's loyalty? To whom?

## After Rabin's Assassination

NOVEMBER 1995

*Prime Minister Yitzhak Rabin was assassinated on November 4, 1995, by a Jewish law student who acted alone. Yigal Amir succeeded in penetrating the security around Rabin—who was leaving a large peace rally in Tel Aviv—and fatally shot the prime minister at close range. The news of the assassination sent shock waves throughout Israel and around the world. The murder was strongly condemned by most parts of Israeli society, despite an already widespread opposition to the Rabin government's policies. The traumatic event became a significant turning point in Israeli politics and the peace process.*

### I

Three bullets ended Yitzhak Rabin's life, and all that his life symbolized. It's as if the image of an entire generation shattered into tiny pieces and the era of the Sabra came to an end.

In all that he did, Rabin was a product of the forge of the elemental experiences that produced the Sabra, the new native Israeli. The biography of this man, who was so often called a traitor, passed through all the archetypical formative stations of the Israeli character—a prominent agricultural boarding school; training on a kibbutz combined with military service in the Palmach, the elite strike force of the nascent Jewish state; the Palmach's first commander's course; the army convoys that supplied besieged Jerusalem during the

War of Independence of 1948; the battle for the Negev, Israel's southern region, in that same war; command of the army in the Six-Day War; and more, throughout Israel's history. This is the DNA of the Israeli identity.

But he wasn't a Sabra only in his peak moments. He was no less a Sabra in his weaknesses and mistakes. An entire generation could look at him as its reflection. They could see what happened to the mythological, idealist, ideal Sabra when his life became entangled in the trivial matters of daily life, in political intrigue, in the temptations of money.

Even his physical appearance could teach us something that we didn't know. This youthful Sabra with the handsome face and the uncombed, wavy hair turned into an adult, and then into an old man. Rabin's very real face allowed us to sense how our ideals and hopes slowly became flesh, became real life, became real time. We walked with him, watching him, as if walking alongside ourselves, each according to his age, and we saw our own image in him.

Then, just when he was at the lowest point of his political career, he began to soar again. To my mind, in accomplishing this astounding turnaround, Rabin returned to the most profound essence of the Sabra character. He displayed an amazing capacity for renewal, and loyalty to the deepest, most manifest interest of Israel and the Jewish people. Most of all, he displayed exceptional courage. Rabin not only changed his political positions. He showed all of us, even the dubious, that we never have to be the victims of our fears, of our preconceptions, of the education we received, or of the circumstances of our lives.

Rabin prevailed over all these, and first and foremost over himself. He overcame a certain tough and unnuanced view of the world. He surmounted the exclusively military reflexes that were so vital to him—and to us—in times of war. In a relatively brief process, he almost re-created himself as a statesman, as a military man, as a man. Even if at times he was not striding with the proper determination and speed toward peace, I wonder how many of us could, at a much younger age and with a less charged and imposing biography, identify at the right moment the opportunity, the birth of a new reality, and act with such resolve in a field of action that was both unfamiliar and not completely comprehensible.

How many of us could have been so victorious over ourselves, over the fears imprinted within us, within our natures?

## II

I was driving yesterday through the Jerusalem Forest, and at one of the turns in the road, on the side, hidden behind a small clump of trees, I saw a man get out of his car and quickly peel off a black-and-red bumper sticker inscribed RABIN IS A MURDERER. What will this man say to his children today? How will he explain to them why he put the bumper sticker on his car and why he tore it off today?

As has happened so many times in history, the gunshots came at the end of a long string of violent words, of provocations and curses, and of incendiary bumper stickers. How did the speakers and cursers and street inciters not understand that at the end of every such chain of events stands a man with a gun, who will add the deadly exclamation point to all those words echoing in his ears?

Our lives in Israel are lives of ongoing violence. The country was born in war, and it has lived with war and terror and occupation. Violence was also part of the Sabra experience, but the Sabra never seems to have been able to assimilate that part of his identity. Perhaps, had more of them managed to resolve this internal contradiction, to comprehend in a profound way the internal toxification that our massive use of force brings upon us, then we might long ago have been living in a different political and social reality. Perhaps yesterday, at the climax of the magnificent and heartwarming Act III, the pistol concealed within us since Act I might not have gone off.

Yitzhak Rabin tried to introduce a profound change here, even though he had, for years, participated in that same use of violence and force. To our detriment, the violence seeped into the entire tissue of our social and private lives. The murderer is a metastasis of the violence, the hatred, the loathing, and the cruelty that we have become accustomed over the years to direct, not only against our enemies, but also against ourselves.

Sometimes it seems that nowhere else in the world are Israelis hated as much as they are here, in our own country, on our own roads, on the beach, in the city streets.

The action that Yitzhak Rabin led was meant, at its most fundamental level, to bring about the end of the violence between us and our enemies, and also our own healing. We have what I would cautiously call the Israeli disease, a constant and deadly nervous condition of hatred within.

It is now clearer than it ever was that peace is necessary for us *primarily for this purpose.* Peace is our chance to live full lives here. Surely, in a harsh reality, without illusions, and with full and painful awareness of all our faces and all our scars. But to live, finally—not only to survive from disaster to disaster. The assassination on Saturday night warns us, in the most shocking way, that from now on the war for peace is a war for our chance to continue to exist, and to develop normally as a nation, as a society, and as human beings.

## When Fear Overcomes Everything

MARCH 1996

*Israel experienced a particularly horrendous wave of terrorism in February and March 1996, during Shimon Peres's brief tenure as prime minister and defense minister after Rabin's assassination. The killing of children in costumes celebrating the Jewish holiday of Purim in Tel Aviv was the cause of much Israeli rage. Hamas claimed the attacks were in retaliation for Israel's liquidation of their master bomb maker, Yehia Ayache. These were the first of the suicide bombings that were to become the archetypal terrorist attack of the years to come.*

This morning, when I woke up my eleven-year-old son, he asked, "Has today's terrorist attack already happened?" My son is scared, as are most of Israel's citizens—during the last two weeks there have been five suicide bombings, in which more than fifty Israelis were killed and hundreds wounded. We have seen horrifying scenes of civilian slaughter of a kind we did not see in our worst wars. People have been crying out: How long will this go on? What kind of peace is this? Even Israelis who have supported the peace process so far have begun losing confidence in it, and the public opinion polls show a sharp rise in support for the political parties of the right. PERES, PERES, taunted the signs at a right-wing demonstration after the attacks, IS THIS WHAT YOUR NEW MIDDLE EAST LOOKS LIKE?

True, the vision and idea seem impotent when you are faced with the stench of scorched flesh and the spilt blood. Fear overwhelms all other thoughts—when you walk down the street, you examine everyone seven times over. Any one of them might be your murderer (and, surprisingly, you discover that almost every single person—even familiar ones—appears sinister in some way). Every decision is liable to be a fateful one. Should I stop for a drink at this stand, or wait to get to the next one? Should I send my two children to school on the same bus? (And then there's the decision over which child to send on the 7:10 and which child on the following bus.) I find myself walking down the main street where I have walked since childhood, the bustling, raucous, somewhat provincial main street of Jerusalem, with my mind ceaselessly smashing this beloved scene into little bits. I keep bidding the familiar farewell. Its impermanence elicits my compassion. Everything is so fragile—the body, routine, family, the fabric of life.

We Israelis are accustomed to living in the vicinity of death. I'll never forget how a young couple once told me about their plans for the future: they'd get married and have three children. Not two, but three. So that if one dies, there will still be two left. This heart-wrenching way of thinking is not foreign to me. It's the product of the unbearable lightness of death that prevails here, a way of seeing things that, in my opinion, is also characteristic of the long-suffering Palestinians. It's precisely the disease that Yitzhak Rabin and Yasir Arafat sought to cure by turning onto the road of peace. Hamas's suicide bombers want to keep the disease alive, and volunteer to spread it. Once, years ago, they hijacked airplanes; today they wish to hijack our future.

It is depressing to think that we are conducting a dialogue of peace with people who have among them spiritual-religious shepherds who enthusiastically send young people to their deaths in order to kill Jews. I cannot comprehend exactly what kind of God these people worship. What God can be proud that His people slaughter little children on their way to a holiday party?

It's also depressing to see that, until now, we hear almost no Palestinian voices condemning these acts of mass murder. Where are you, Palestinian intellectuals who should be denouncing this? Where are the writers, where are the humanists? Don't you understand that this is no longer just Israel's war? After all, Hamas will want to impose its fanatic worldview on you moderate, secular people as well.

Tempers are high in Israel. People are demanding revenge and the annulment of the entire peace process. But even in this difficult hour, we must remember that this is the only way open to us if we want to live. We've already tried the alternative route, the one opposed to peace, for decades, and we still bear its physical and spiritual scars. The peace process will be long and painful, and apparently not all of us will survive it, but there are no quick solutions to such a complex and lengthy conflict. Israel and the moderate Palestinians help each other all along the way, because peace is the only state that can ensure that at least our grandchildren—I no longer believe that it will apply to our children—will be able to live a life of security, of normalcy, of blessed routine. A life in which young couples will want to have three children, maybe more, simply because it is a joy to raise them.

# Open Letter to Prime Minister Benjamin Netanyahu

OCTOBER 1996

*Benjamin Netanyahu, leader of the right-wing Likud Party, beat Labor's Shimon Peres in the general elections on May 29, 1996, by a razor-thin margin of 51 percent to 49 percent. The election results clearly reflected Israel's deep division on the issue of national security. After initially declaring that he would not convene with Arafat, Netanyahu met the Palestinian leader at the Erez roadblock in the Gaza Strip on October 6, 1996.*

Mr. Prime Minister,

The moment of truth has arrived, like it or not. The talks that will commence in a few hours will ostensibly address only specific points of disagreement. But in the new state of affairs that you have created, these talks might well be the last opportunity to get the peace process back on track, without forcing us all, Israelis and Palestinians, to endure another lengthy bloodbath.

Reality lies before you—read it. Israel cannot long maintain a situation in which the Palestinians live in frustration and rage. Any solution that does not give the Palestinians hope for a state of their own, within a reasonable period of time, will intensify their frustration and rage. Do you perceive some new way to resolve this dilemma?

There is no other way but the way begun by the late Yitzhak Rabin and by Shimon Peres. We have no alternative reality, and there is no half-solution. Most of the world's countries have recognized this, as has most of Palestinian society. Even most of the Israeli nation has already begun to adjust, if without great enthusiasm, to the idea of sharing the land between the Jordan River and the Mediterranean. Five or ten years from now, after hundreds or thousands have lost their lives, there will be two countries here. They will not have great mutual trust, but they will fear the alternative. They won't relinquish their dreams, but they will understand the clear advantages of accepting each other's existence.

Is there really no other way? There is, of course. It's the way of hostility and humiliation and occupation. But we've already tried that, and we've seen where it led us. If we go down that path again, we will find it to be more violent and horrible than ever before. We've already come to realize that the more time Israel tries to buy, the higher the price it has to pay in concessions, in blood, and in internal disintegration. For those who choose life, there is currently only one way—that of the great and painful concession, of the calculated risk.

Rarely does the world present us with such a drastic and clear choice. Any step that does not lead directly and uncompromisingly to this one road leads to the other. Convoluted words and phrases can no longer create new conditions. The writing is already on the wall, and it is written, as the poet Yehuda Amichai said (in another context), in three languages—Hebrew, Arabic, and Death.

Three days ago you issued a heartfelt and, in your words, sincere appeal to the Palestinians, and spoke of your desire for real peace. But in all honesty, Mr. Prime Minister, if you were this morning a Palestinian who desired peace, would the offers that Israel has been making over the last three months seem like "real peace"?

I pose to you another question, which is the core of the matter, in my opinion. Does the vision that you are offering us Israelis today really include our great and only chance of recovering, finally, from the historical error that has drawn our blood and all the good we could have within us? What is the point of aspiring to lead Israel at this time, in this situation, if you are not able to promise Israeli citizens the opportunity to end the occupation of another nation?

Mr. Prime Minister, the late Yitzhak Rabin entered the Oslo process knowing that he also represented the half of the nation that feared this peace. The Oslo Accords actually reflect the anxieties of this half of the Israeli people. This morning, and in the days to come, when you brief your representatives, when you go to meet Yasir Arafat again, and when you face difficult decisions, please do not forget that you also represent those of the other half of the nation, who, despite their trepidation, are not prepared to continue this way. For these people, the very desire to live is being taken from them because they have spent the last thirty years in circumstances that they view as deformed, immoral, unjust, and, especially, not safe. It's this half of the nation that will have difficulty understanding why it is being called to fight, very soon, when the secure peace you have promised becomes a slaughtered peace.

You represent those millions of Israelis as well. You must give them voice; their hopes must be realized in your actions; their courage must beat within you.

If the peace that you intend to lay before the Palestinians and Israelis today is not substantially different from what you have proposed so far, there is no reason to even send your delegates to the Erez roadblock for negotiations. Better that you, too, remain in your office, to prepare the nation and the army for what lies ahead. But if you want true peace—not a peace of virtual, imaginary reality, not a compromise that answers only to your own needs—you must begin, at last, to work for it today.

The answer to all the questions I have raised here will be given in the next few days. It will be an unambiguous, definite answer, and we eagerly await it with anticipation and hope. We'll know how to identify and decipher the answer no matter how you spin it. You have boasted that you have won thirty debating competitions in the American school you attended, but to answer the questions that the country's majority puts to you this morning, you do not need convoluted rebuttals, neither for Israelis nor for Palestinians. You need only one word. Are you or are you not ushering in change, toward real peace? Is it or is it not a peace that will have a partner? Can you say, in all sincerity, that as the leader of this nation, you have this week chosen life?

# No Peace, No Security

JULY 1997

*Two coordinated suicide bombings on July 30, 1997, in the Jerusalem Mahaneh Yehuda market, left 16 people dead and 180 wounded. Five weeks later, central Jerusalem was hit again with another major terrorist attack carried out by three Hamas suicide bombers. On October 1, 1997, Israel acceded to pressure from Jordan and released the spiritual leader of Hamas, Sheikh Ahmed Yassin.*

Two explosions that slayed so many Israelis and wounded nearly two hundred have also punctured the strange bubble in which Israelis have been floating this past year.

Despair and paralysis pervaded the bubble, as did, in particular, a desire not to know what is really happening. In the period since Benjamin Netanyahu came to power, it seemed as if no one in Israel truly understood the reality that the prime minister was creating with his sleights of hand, and the consequences of that reality. The situation has repeatedly reached the brink of explosion, yet each time, at the last minute, the peace process has been rescued. Not in order to surge forward toward realization, but rather again to tread water.

The explosions in Jerusalem's central open-air market woke all of us up from the absurd illusion that things could stay as they are indefinitely. The explosions also proved the irrelevance of Netanyahu's campaign slogan "Making a secure peace," and showed that without peace there is also no security.

True, under the Rabin and Peres governments there were also mass murders of innocent Israelis by Palestinian suicide bombers, but then, at least, it was clear that a genuine peace would gradually reduce the number and power of those who support such acts. Today it is hard to speak of the Palestinians having any hope. The majority of Israelis do not realize the depth of Palestinian despair and humiliation caused by Israeli government policies. Under these circumstances, it is now clear, Israeli lives will be as intolerable as Palestinian lives.

The two peoples have not learned anything. Israel condemns the use of force and terror, but itself exerts the full force of its political, economic, and military might to suffocate the Palestinians in the occupied territories and to extinguish any glimmer of hope they may have. Arafat, in his distress, but also as a result of his own cynical calculations, is not prepared to withdraw his own cards of force and violence. He has taken great care not to make any serious effort to fight terrorism and Hamas's supporters (only two weeks ago, senior Palestinian officers and policemen from the Palestinian Authority were caught on their way to committing a terrorist attack in Israel). Each time he speaks publicly, he takes care to leave the option of war open.

On the face of it, one might have thought that in such a savage region, only the language of violence could ensure political gain. But that, too, is an illusion that we should have long ago abandoned. Violence justifies more violence and makes pursuers of peace despair all the more.

Today is especially bitter and depressing, because only four years ago we could envision how despicable acts such as this explosion might be gradually relegated to the past. We almost realized a dream, but it has evaporated. Again we are caught up in the spiral of violence we were born into. We want peace, but it seems that many, among both peoples, are still not ripe for it. The pessimists in Israel like to say that only another round of violence will make the two sides come to their senses, but now even that seems optimistic fantasy. Another war will only make the positions of each side more extreme, and will drag more people into the cycle of hatred and revenge.

The dead lie before us, innocent dead, pawns in the hands of incompetent and cynical leaders. It seems that this last explosion requires us to examine reality as it is. Israelis and Palestinians cannot on their own reach an agreement that will ensure lasting peace. They are hostages of their history and psychology, and have lost their ability to save themselves. If there are still other countries that care about what is happening in this corner of the world, they should take action to force the leaders on both sides to begin talking seriously. The American tactic of "letting the sides stew in their own juices" is not effective. Neither is European caution called for. We now need determined pressure on both sides, especially on Israel, which holds most of the cards. Pressure that will take account of the justified fears of the two peoples and of their actual needs. Pressure that may just save the Israelis and the Palestinians from themselves.

## Whose Life Is It, Anyway?

SEPTEMBER 1998

*This article was written on the eve of the Jewish New Year.*

This week, with the Jewish year drawing to a close, is a time for making personal and communal assessments. A seemingly strange question came to me in this context: Are there any Israelis today who feel that they are living the life they would like to live?

Also, how has it happened that Israeli reality is, more than anything else, a depressing sequence of compromises and anxieties and apathy and fatalism?

And the government, the one elected by the majority—who, actually, does it represent today?

In other words, would Israelis today, even a handful, on the left or on the right, give their votes to any leader whose platform promised voters the current state of affairs?

"We've got a wonderful country," Prime Minister Benjamin Netanyahu thunders at every opportunity. He's right—we really do have a wonderful country, but why does it seem like a dream that is steadily fading? And why does almost every large sector of the population—the religious, the secular, the settlers, members of Peace Now, the Russians, the Ethiopians, the ultraorthodox, the unemployed, the Israeli

Arabs—see itself as a persecuted minority, living under a hostile regime? And why do so many Israelis feel that an ever-expanding abyss of alienation stretches between them and their own country?

Apparently, there's something mesmerizing about that abyss. It's a fact: nearly six million people are being sucked into it without protesting much, without frequent, huge demonstrations, without vigils at every street corner. There are no individual hunger strikes, or any other legitimate acts of civil disobedience. There's not even a single television satire worthy of the name.

But the sense that something has passed us by doesn't let go, the feeling that something precious and rare is slipping through our fingers, irrevocably. Perhaps, for that reason, Israelis are becoming more bitter and resentful by the year, displaying a specific kind of hostility toward one another, like that of prisoners sharing a cell, like partners in a failing business.

How little sympathy and understanding we have, even for other Israelis who don't belong to our own group. With what rage, or derision, we relate to the real, authentic pain of Israelis who are not "us." As if our automatic and long-standing refusal to recognize at least some of the Palestinian claims, lest any of the justice of our own cause be appropriated from us, has seeped into our most inner selves and set entirely awry our common sense and natural family instincts. At times it seems as if what Jews do to other Jews in this country would be defined in any other country as nothing less than anti-Semitism.

Those who return to Israel after a long absence are generally amazed by the tremendous development of the cities, the roads, and the malls, but are taken aback by the people themselves—the brutality, the vulgarity, and the insensitivity. Those who live here have long since ceased being surprised by this. Within an astoundingly short time our young, friendly, bold country has undergone mental processes of accelerated aging. With a peculiar enthusiasm, Israel has taken on a manner that is rigid, suspicious, dejected, and, more than anything else, lacking confidence in its ability to change, to be re-created into a better tomorrow.

As in an old science fiction story, an entire nation has been caught in a time warp, where it spins round and round, doomed to relive all the worst evils of its tragic history. Maybe, for that reason, when Israel is at the height of its military power, Israelis themselves lose their ability to act. They become nonpersons, victims in fact; only, this time they are their own victims.

Six million Israelis have allowed their mind, their will, and their judgment to degenerate into infuriating criminal passivity. They have lost their ability to distinguish between right and wrong. Most of all, they have lost the healthy instinct that should rouse and shake them, that will remind them what their goals and needs are, their most profound ones as a people and as a society.

An entire nation is in a coma. It is as if the people have voluntarily anesthetized themselves, suspended their discernment, so as not to face up to the quiet horror of their condition.

Just to think, for example, that the government is funneling more money into construction in the settlements in the territories, which will complicate and convolute the situation even further and make any political solution impossible.

Just to think, that an entire nation has forfeited its future, its only chance of getting out of the trap it is in, simply to humor the messianic, militaristic urges of a few thousand—

no more—fanatics who insist on pushing themselves into Hebron, Nablus, and the Gaza Strip.

And, worst of all, consider that we have been ruling over another nation for thirty-one years, even though we have the alternative of not doing so.

But that's already become a cliché, "to rule over another nation." The Israeli eye is already trained to skip over the small items in the newspaper: the Palestinian babies dying at roadblocks, the children fainting from thirst in the refugee camps because Israeli officials control the water supply, thousands of families whose homes are bulldozed on the grounds of being "illegal construction." Who can face up to all this nauseating detail? Who can acknowledge that this is actually happening? *That it is really happening to us?*

As in a fairy tale, as in a nightmare: Hush . . . the entire kingdom has fallen asleep.

That is, people are awake. They move, produce sounds, travel, enjoy themselves, do business. Lots of activity, lots of noise.

Yet underneath all that, the same gnawing corrosion of the heart, the feeling that something here is hollow, that its movement is but inertial, that it is disconnected, excised from its essence.

We've been so wonderful at putting ourselves to sleep, at suspending our understanding and our will, that even those who oppose the government's policy don't have the strength to really do anything against it.

And so it happens that, despite the conspicuous void in this country's leadership, the opposition is unable to produce a single person who can respond to the profound need for restoration, someone who could sweep along the masses simply by, finally, offering them *anything*, a way, a chance, an awakening.

Perhaps Israel is now paying the heavy price of too many years of stubbornness, of opposition to compromise and refusal to understand reality as it is. Perhaps something really horrible has happened to us. Perhaps the peace process came to us a bit too late.

Because when you keep rejecting something for so long, when you so much don't want something, you are liable, in the end, *not to want anything.* In other words, you are liable to lose your will itself. So the result is a nation that has spent years investing huge amounts of energy in not wanting and has now reached a state in which it is so passive that anything can be inflicted upon it, anything at all.

Maybe I'm wrong. Maybe everything really is operating as it should, according to a well-thought-out plan, a plan of genius that is beyond my comprehension.

I may well be wrong, but I know that something in me is dying. I no longer have that spark inside that life here always ignited in me. With all my criticism and all my pain, I also had joy, even pride, about belonging to such a unique, unprecedented human enterprise. So full of promise.

I am trying to comfort myself with the hope that, despite it all, a change will happen soon (not a withdrawal of a few miles here or there; rather, a profound change in the way the world is seen). After all, where there are living beings, immobility cannot be sustained for long. Perhaps we will soon be released from this evil spell. But I also know that there are parts of the soul, the individual soul and the collective soul, that cannot be suspended "for the time being," or only "until circumstances change." Because afterward, you cannot reclaim those parts.

When the change finally takes place—and let us hope that it will be a change for the better, not another war or popular uprising or who-knows-what—when we emerge from the cocoon that encloses us, it is liable to be too late. We may make a few political gains, we may well retain a few strategic hills and roadblocks, but the main thing—the spark that will truly ensure we maintain our identity and continuity—could already be lost.

May we wake up at last, may we stop straying through this nightmare, which is no one's dream.

*Shana Tova*, Happy New Year.

# Beware, Opportunity Ahead

SEPTEMBER 1999

*In a landslide victory over Netanyahu, Labor leader Ehud Barak won the May 18, 1999, Israeli general elections. The former army general vowed to renew the peace talks and declared that he was ready to negotiate land for peace. On September 4 of that same year, Barak and Arafat met in an Egyptian Sinai resort to sign the Sharm el-Sheikh Memorandum on Implementation Timeline of Outstanding Commitments of Agreements Signed and the Resumption of Permanent Status Negotiations. The issues agreed upon included the gradual transfer of areas to Palestinian control, security, and safe passage between the West Bank and the Gaza Strip.*

The Israelis and the Palestinians didn't dance in the streets after this new agreement. The two nations are already well aware of the disparity between, on the one hand, the euphoria often characteristic of the formal language used in signing ceremonies and, on the other hand, the actual execution of the agreements. The latter is generally done without enthusiasm, in a petty and even resentful way.

The present agreement contains no dramatic change from the Wye Plantation agreement, achieved eleven months ago and much trumpeted in Washington.

But it would be a mistake to judge this agreement only on

the basis of the apparent successes that one side or the other scored. The great achievement is that the peace process, which Benjamin Netanyahu suspended and slowed down as much as he could for nearly three years, is again back on track.

This agreement and the way it was achieved are in large part the agenda that Israel's new prime minister, Ehud Barak, has presented to his people. When we examine it, we find a few very clear pieces of information. The first, and most important, is that Barak does, in fact, intend to lead Israel into a historic peace with the Palestinians. The second piece of information is that the price of this peace—handing territories over to the Palestinians—still looks nearly intolerable to Barak. He is not necessarily willing to pay it. The third piece of information arising from the way Barak conducted the negotiations is that, despite the great historic opportunity, both sides continue to treat each other with suspicion and animosity, as they became accustomed to doing during the Netanyahu period.

Barak most certainly has a bold and revolutionary vision of a new Middle East, and unlike previous Israeli leaders, he can carry it out without encountering too much opposition from the great majority of Israelis. Yet Barak suffers from the same infirmity as his predecessors. He lacks sensitivity to the problems of his partner—Arafat—and to the Palestinian people's terrible distress and years of frustration.

Arafat, for his part, still seems to be having trouble believing that he is facing the best partner he can hope for under the present circumstances. He is haggling with Barak just as he did with Netanyahu, stubbornly holding his ground on small details. In doing so, he is contributing to the dissolution of the chance for a true, profound change in the relationship between the two peoples.

We now have an entire year ahead of us before reaching a final agreement. During this year the two sides will have to resolve the approximately 450 problems and disputes that now divide them. Is this possible? At first glance, it seems impossible. But perhaps we should see it differently. The conflict between the two peoples has almost run itself out. The majority in both nations are weary of war. The Israelis and Palestinians already know in their hearts, more or less, what dreams they will have to give up and what they will gain.

Only two things remain a riddle. We don't know how much time will be lost until the solutions are found and how much blood will be spilled by then. Ehud Barak has, with the vision of a great leader—or with appalling naïveté—announced: Within a single year we will have a permanent status agreement.

The heart hopes that there is good sense behind this move of his, in definitively cutting the tangled Gordian knot between the Israelis and the Palestinians. But that same heart is well acquainted with the two peoples who are party to this conflict. It knows their suspicious, cynical character, their self-destructive tendencies, and the fear that has become second nature to them—the fear of believing that there is hope for another kind of life in the Middle East.

Despite this, I allow myself to celebrate today—because, despite all the doubts and the sorrow over all the gratuitous insults they have hurled at each other, it's clear to me today, more than it ever has been, that the hundred-year-old conflict between them has been heading in the right direction these last few years. The process of accommodation has survived repeated blows from both sides, and this may be evidence that, inside the armor that all of us in this region have become accustomed to living in, a hunger for life still has us in its grasp.

## Expulsion of the Cave Dwellers

DECEMBER 1999

*On November 16, 1999, the Israeli Army evacuated 750 Palestinian villagers whose families had been living in mountainside caves near Hebron in the West Bank since the 1830s. The Israeli Supreme Court ruled in March 2000 that the cave dwellers could return to their homes pending a final determination in the case. In July 2001, the Israeli Army raided cave dwellings and expelled hundreds of people again. The struggle between the State of Israel and the cave dwellers currently awaits a final court decision. Israeli and international peace and human rights organizations mounted a massive campaign in support of the cave dwellers.*

"I was born here in this cave," said Mahmoud Hamamdeh, "and here my father was born and here my seven children were born. Give me a three-story house? Don't want it. Give me a hotel? Don't want it. Only here. And what has happened?"

What happened is that, three weeks ago, several dozen army armored personnel carriers and jeeps showed up. The soldiers surrounded the village of al-Mufkara on the southern flank of Mt. Hebron, cordoned off the field containing Hamamdeh's cave and the caves of other families, as well as some tents and corrugated metal shacks, and ordered the people to leave the homes they'd been living in for decades.

Afterward the soldiers went into the caves, piled up mattresses, woolen blankets, buckets, and sacks of barley, and scuffled with frightened children and with women screaming in panic. Our soldiers opened the plywood door of the adjacent cave, where the sheep and the chickens were kept, and shooed out the livestock. They knew that their owners would run after the sheep, to keep them from getting lost in the desert, and so they did.

After a commotion that lasted for a while, the commander could report that the mission had been accomplished, or some such euphemism. The cave dwellers' belongings were impounded, and they were told, in accordance with regulations, and in absolutely clear language, that they could receive their personal effects only by paying a certain sum of money, a hundred or so dollars—that's all.

Then the soldiers returned to the caves, just to take one last look, because they'd never ever seen anything like this. They scouted out the crevices and were astounded at how human beings could, in the final month of the twentieth century, live in moldy, dark caves, between damp stone walls, on ground covered with ash and goat turds. Afterward, all our soldiers returned safely to their base.

There are two explanations for this action. When the residents of Ma'on Farm, a squatters' site set up by Israeli settlers in the West Bank, were evacuated by the army, the settlers were promised "balance." That is, action would be taken to harm the Palestinians as well. So they shouldn't be too pleased, those Arabs. Another explanation: the army needs the field as yet another firing range for military training. (In May 1999, land belonging to sixty-nine villages in the West Bank was similarly categorized as a "closed military zone," and no one was permitted to enter.)

In the three intervening weeks, the inhabitants of al-Mufkara have been wandering around their village befuddled, forbidden to enter. They've found partial refuge in the adjacent village of Tweineh, which is no more than a gaggle of houses and some lean-tos. But Tweineh can't take in all the refugees from the caves—almost 250 human beings—and the parched fields can't feed the additional flocks. And there is already tension between the guests and the hosts. Says Hamamdeh: "At night, when it's cold, they take us into their homes, but during the day they tell us to go far away."

I stand there, at the entrance to a cave, I see and I hear, and I can't really grasp it. What is happening here? How can it be that we, each and every citizen of Israel, are signed on to this operation? We fund it with our taxes, and carry it out through the sons and daughters we send to serve in the army. What is the connection between the army we knew and the institution that commits such an act against defenseless people?

There is no argument that if the country is in a war of survival, it is permitted to use all means necessary to protect itself.

But now? From our position of strength? Israel, the great military power, against those people out there in the fields, in the caves? How low can you go, and how cruel can you get?

Last Friday, in bone-chilling cold, on the main road at the edge of Tweineh, a woman sat next to a pile of mattresses. At her side, clinging to her, were several children, toddlers among them, wearing thin clothes. When she saw our little delegation, her eyes showed no flicker of life or interest. Later, without much hope, she urged one of the children to cough loudly, to elicit our pity. The boy, about nine years old, looked at us, shrugged his shoulders, and stubbornly remained silent.

At that moment he had more self-respect than I could find for myself as an Israeli.

If I could directly address Israel's prime minister, Ehud Barak, I would say to him, Sir, I want to believe that you didn't know exactly what was taking place there. That you had no idea how one signature of yours on a document would be translated into reality and affect individuals. I have no doubt that, had you witnessed what I saw there, in the field, in the caves, you would have canceled the decree and ordered that these people be immediately reinstated in their homes.

There is a struggle over territory, true, and we are in the midst of negotiations over borders, absolutely. But beyond this there is the matter of the boundary that a man makes for himself, the final boundary beyond which a person and an entire people lose their self-respect, and in the end their identity as well. There are deeds that an army—especially one that once bore the banner of "purity of arms"—does not do. Because in performing them, it ceases to defend the nation whose agent it is and begins to act counter to that nation's most profound interests.

Mr. Prime Minister, I'll say it in the simplest possible terms: It is not fair to bully these helpless people. These are not the values that you, sir, were raised on, and it is not the education you passed on to generations of soldiers. This is not what we reflected on when, years ago, we studied the prophet Nathan's parable of the poor man's ewe lamb that the rich man stole.

It is not too late. That is, it is definitely late. Because three weeks like these, staying outside in the cold, humiliated, will not be erased from the memory of the refugees. But something can still be repaired. Today. Right now. You don't need to ponder over it too long. There's no need to consult various advisors. This is something that a person recognizes from within, from the deepest place inside. If you give the order to restore these people to their homes, no one will consider it as surrender to Palestinian pressure. On the contrary, they will see it as an act of loyalty to your fundamental values and those of the nation you lead. Sometimes a little repair, even Tikkun like this—in the midst of the moral chaos in which Israel finds itself today—can remind its citizens of what they once were, and what they hope someday to become, when this passes, this storm that sends our compasses awry.

## Leave Lebanon Now

FEBRUARY 2000

*Ehud Barak promised, as part of his election campaign, to withdraw the Israeli Army from southern Lebanon within a year—after eighteen years of occupation. Grassroots organizations persisted in their pressure on the government to fulfill this controversial promise.*

Six Israeli soldiers have been killed by Hezbollah attacks in Lebanon in ten days. The Israeli government has decided on a tough response. Israeli Air Force fighter planes have bombed power plants deep inside Lebanese territory. Hezbollah has continued to attack Israeli outposts in southern Lebanon, and a flare-up seems imminent.

But, in fact, it doesn't really matter what Israel's tough response in Lebanon will be. The entire process is preordained, and it is only an illusion to believe that Israel controls or initiates any part of it.

Time and time again, for over twenty years now, our leaders have brought us to a Lebanese blind alley in which we are forced to act precisely contrary to our real needs.

This time, too, apparently, we will react the same way. We'll once again behave like the drowning man whose frantic flailing sucks him deeper and deeper into the water.

Why does it have to be this way? Why does it sometimes seem as if we Israelis are doomed to make this error by our very nature? That it's the result of our too finely honed instincts, which in the end bring more disasters upon us?

We do not acknowledge the failure of our continued, pointless presence in Lebanon. We are not admitting that our deterrent force decays further with each additional day there. We do not accept that there is no military solution to the Lebanon problem. Instead of facing up boldly to these facts, it's much easier for us to turn our frustration and humiliation into a great fist and to strike out, hard.

But when you look back today on the many years during which our soldiers have participated in this bloody ritual, your heart breaks. It's the thought that perhaps most of the retaliatory operations were no more than superfluous and dangerous acts of revenge, an automatic outlet for the well-known overconfidence of military men—as well as of politicians who were once military men—who know no other way but force.

Yes, we realize that they are undoubtedly levelheaded, responsible, sober men, but what's to be done if their sobriety and levelheadedness prompt them to take two or three steps that repeat themselves in a sort of mechanical routine? At most, they can "suspend" or "examine" their response until what seems to them an appropriate moment, and then, as usual, they react with force and aggression, and recommence for the thousandth time the vicious, bloody circle.

But how is it possible, ask many Israelis who have already come to terms with the idea of a withdrawal, how can we leave this way, with our tail between our legs? How can we allow Hezbollah to humiliate us so?

Because, the answer is, there is no longer any alternative. We've got to get out. It's not important how the retreat is called or what other people may call it. In any case, we should keep in mind that this won't be the first time that Israeli soldiers have left Lebanon without completing their mission. In 1986, after four years of plodding slowly through the Lebanese mud, Israel withdrew from Lebanon, finally understanding that the price it was paying in human life was too high.

Nor is there any longer a genuine need to deal with the "public relations" of such a withdrawal. Everyone, in Israel and the world, knows the truth. Israel will be able to exert its deterrent force far better from within its borders, with a much greater sense of justice and in national unity. We've got to get out now.

*Get out.* Because we are conquerors, and because throughout history an army that was stationed in an occupied land, imprisoned for all intents and purposes in outposts and trenches, has never succeeded in fighting for any length of time against mobile forces, even if much less powerful.

*Get out.* Because the army of a democratic country, whose actions are restricted by law and by accepted moral norms, can never defeat a guerrilla army fighting for its land, supported by the local population, knowing that justice is on its side.

*Get out.* Not because Hezbollah is a fairer or more moral adversary than we are. It is an organization that cynically trades in the body parts of its enemies, that has no compunctions about using women and children as human shields in shooting attacks, and that does not hesitate to launch indiscriminate attacks on civilian settlements over the border. But Israel's position against Hezbollah will be much more determined and ethical if it redeploys on the international border, ends the state of occupation, and denies every enemy the right to act against it. If, after the withdrawal, Hezbollah attacks the inhabitants of northern Israel, Israel will have every right to act against Lebanon, a sovereign country.

*Get out.* Because, in doing so, Israel will deny President Assad his main bargaining card—his ability to use Hezbollah as a proxy to attack Israel's soldiers and so apply intolerable pressure on Israel during the negotiations over Israel's withdrawal from the Golan Heights.

*Get out.* Not in July, which Prime Minister Barak has set as his target date. After all, July is just an arbitrary and artificial deadline set a year ago as part of Barak's election campaign. If it can be done in July, why can't it be done next week? Why not start the retreat today?

*Get out.* Evacuate the outposts, bring our soldiers home, redeploy on the border.

*Get out.* Swallow our questionable pride. Stop feeding the miserable hubristic fire within us with ever more young soldiers. Every soldier killed now is an unnecessary victim of military arrogance. The same is true of every Lebanese civilian who is hurt. We need to state explicitly: It's not the doubts and protests being heard on Israel's home front that are destroying the Israeli Army's chances of success there. It's the sense of error and pointlessness, and the feeling that the fighting will never end.

*Get out.* We began this war defeated, and if Barak gets us out now, it will be his first great victory as prime minister.

But to achieve that, he will have to recognize that we've lost this war. We are defeated. We can say it out loud—and not die of it.

Of *that* you don't die.

*On May 22, 2000, Israel withdrew its forces to the international border with Lebanon in a quick forty-eight hour operation—two months before the original deadline set for withdrawal by Barak.*

# The Pope's Visit to Israel

MARCH 2000

*Pope John Paul II made a historic official visit to the State of Israel on March 20, 2000, as part of a wider, millennium-commemorating visit to the holy Christian sites of the region. He was accompanied by tens of thousands of pilgrims. During his weeklong stay, the Pope visited the Christian holy sites both in Israel and in the Palestinian Authority territories, as well as sacred Muslim and Jewish sites and secular sites like Yad Vashem and a Palestinian refugee camp. The visit elicited much attention and interest around the Christian world and among Israelis and Arabs.*

## DAY ONE: THE POPE ARRIVES

An Israeli sits in front of his television set in his home in Jerusalem and watches the Pope arrive in his country.

This person is not religious. Religious ceremonies are foreign to him, and religious institutions in particular are foreign to him. He is very Jewish, and he respects those whose religious fervor burns in their hearts, but he himself has not performed what Kierkegaard called "the leap of faith."

For a few days he's been telling himself that this visit, historic as it is, will certainly neither move nor impress him. He's been explaining to himself that the Pope's visit is of no relevance to him, to his day-to-day routine, to the immediate problems of his private life, or to the political and moral dilemmas that his country has been agonizing over for decades. But when the airplane lands in Israel and the Pope emerges atop the stairway leading down to the tarmac, something suddenly happens.

The Israeli looks at the Pope, an old man, bent and burdened with years, weighted down with experience and the vicissitudes of life. Real sorrow, personal and very human, is also evident in his everyman's face. He gazes at the Pope and suddenly sees, as if by an epiphany, what the Pope himself sees, perhaps: the State of Israel. The reality, both symbolic and concrete, of a country born after two thousand years of exile, religious persecutions, inquisitions, blood libels, pogroms, and the Holocaust.

The man in the armchair isn't in any way resentful about this. He does not in any way see Israel as reprisal for what the Gentiles have done to the Jews, under the leadership and inspiration of most of this current Pope's predecessors.

The opposite is true. In the meditative, profound gaze of the Pope he sees the marvel and the opportunity of the Jewish state. He sees the Jewish people's life force for revival and renewal, which in these difficult times is the source of the great hope that Israel can save itself from the curse of war and attain peace.

The Israeli sitting and watching television fidgets uncomfortably in his chair. He really had had no intention of being carried away by such "historic" sentiments. Nor had he had any intention of reopening old accounts with either the Christian world or the Christian religion. Keeping such score would not, in any case, repair anything, and who today has the strength to peer again into the darkness in which Jewish-Christian relations have been conducted over the last two thousand years?

But then the Pope passes before the honor guard of Israeli soldiers. Bent over, leaning on his cane, deep in his own thoughts, he moves past the strapping armed men, who embody an ironic reversal of ancient stereotypes. The man in the armchair, who is no great fan of armies of any kind, reflects to himself that had any Jews of the last forty generations seen this Jewish military honor guard—even his own father, who fled Europe only seventy years earlier—they would not have believed their eyes. Then the Israeli suddenly comprehends, more than he had allowed himself to do up to this moment, that the restrained, well-planned ceremony is a thin veneer of formality, behind which seethes an entire history. It is a cruel, primal, deep open wound, but maybe now, finally, there is a new opportunity, the first of its type, to heal it.

Then the Israeli national anthem is played. There's no way of knowing whether its words have been translated for John Paul II. Perhaps they ought to be explained here. They speak of hope—the Jews' two-thousand-year hope to establish a free nation in their own land, the land of Zion and Jerusalem.

Then the Pope speaks. He conveys fine and moving thoughts. This brave man, who had the courage to change the Church's position toward Israel and Judaism. He speaks of his spiritual journey here, and a thought about what this great journey can become steals into the Israeli's heart: a journey of elucidation and study, of identification and remorse, a religious and physical journey traversing all the terrible stations we have passed, Jews and Christians, human beings, men, women, and children; a journey to the beginning, from which will, perhaps, begin a new future, a life that is more human and more full of possibilities. This will certainly not happen in one short week. But it can begin here.

### DAY TWO: VISIT TO A REFUGEE CAMP

The Israeli and Palestinian officials were worried and tense as they sat and measured each word of the Pope's speech. Would he depart from the text that had been prepared and agreed to by all parties? Would he refer to the status of Jerusalem? Would he mention the Palestinian demand for a return to the 1967 borders? In the struggle between the two peoples, each gain by one side is still perceived as a defeat for the other. But beyond the words that were said, something deeper was becoming evident. The Israelis and the Palestinians look now like two inimical brothers, modern incarnations of Jacob and Esau, waiting for the blessing of their father. Each brother eyes what the other receives, and has faith in the magical power of the blessing.

I wonder whether the Pope—in his talks with this and that side—was able to comprehend the extent to which their long struggle has made them eerily similar to each other. Both have the same, almost hysterical sensitivity to what other people say and think about them. There's the same manic-depressive excitability, the same need for any former enemy to love them, really love them. They share a potent self-destructive instinct, a compulsion to trip themselves up, and a bitter gravity that is nearly devoid of faith in any promise or hope.

Precisely because the Pope took care not to enter the political minefield, he was able to pronounce some important truths that have almost been forgotten after years of conflict. He spoke of the simple human suffering of millions of refugees, of the pointlessness and inexplicability of this ongoing misery. He reminded those people that their plight does not make them less deserving. With a few simple words he restored to them the honor that the "situation" has stolen from them. And, in passing, he also spoke of the responsibility that all the leaders in the Middle East have for this suffering. I believe that this wholesale indictment was intentional. It's not just Israel's leaders who bear responsibility for the refugees' misery. The leaders of the Arab world do as well. The wealthy Arab countries could long ago have alleviated the refugees' day-to-day distress to some extent, but they preferred to preserve their misery and to cement their suffering in the ugly setting of the refugee camps.

In the Pope's visit to the Deheisheh refugee camp, there was, however, something more important. In conversations I've had with Palestinians, I've often heard them say that they are now paying the price of the persecutions that the Jews suffered from the Christians. "We," say the Palestinians, "are the victims of victims." They often say that the fears that history has instilled into the Jewish soul have made it impossible for Israel to ever feel fully secure. The result, say the Palestinians, is that there can never be true peace.

I reminded them in these conversations that the Arab world has never shown any genuine goodwill toward the tiny Jewish refugee state, and that Israel is not exactly surrounded by the Salvation Army. Even today, I point out, you can still hear Arab radio stations broadcasting calls for the destruction of the "Zionist entity."

But there can be no doubt that the Jewish people's tragic past—a past for which the Church is largely responsible—has created some of the convoluted psychological complexities that make it very difficult for Israel to act today with more courage and largesse, with greater confidence in the Arabs.

From this point of view, the fates of the three religions, and of the Israelis, the Palestinians, and the Catholic Church, are tangled up in a tortuous and tragic knot. When I saw the Pope in the narrow streets of Deheisheh, when I saw him bless the children, the fourth generation of misery, I felt how right this visit was, this visit into the wound; how important was this direct contact with plain human suffering. Redemption will not come, of course, from this short visit, but as an Israeli, I also see recognition of the Catholic Church's obligation to try to loosen, carefully and delicately, the noose that is strangling millions of Israelis and Palestinians.

### DAY THREE: YAD VASHEM

Today, after the ceremony of the Yad Vashem Holocaust memorial, even the most out-and-out cynics must realize how the Pope's visit to Israel touches the foundation of our identity, our most primal emotions.

In their planning of the visit, the parties seem to have thought mostly about abstract symbols, the big images. Yet now, during the visit itself, symbols and human beings are melding time and again; abstract ideas are mixing with tears and wounds and human fragility.

So it was when the Pope spoke of the suffering of the Jews, and so it was when he met with people from his hometown in Poland, with the woman that he himself bore on his back out of the ghetto, to whom he gave a slice of bread and whom he saved from death. And so it was when he stood, head bowed, and communed with the memory of the victims.

Allow me to tell a brief story, a private one. A very dear member of my family, a survivor of the Treblinka death camp, arrived at my wedding with a bandage on her forearm.

She was covering her tattooed number so as not to mar the celebration with a memento of the Holocaust. I remember how I was unable to take my eyes off that bandage. I understood then, very sharply, how much all of us here in Israel are always walking on a surface as thin as that bandage, under which lies a void that threatens, every moment, to drag down our daily lives, our illusion of routine.

I was reminded of that feeling again yesterday, when, at the ceremony, they read a letter that a Jewish woman named Jennia wrote to the woman who hid her son, Michael. The mother asked that he not forget to wear his pajamas at night, and pleaded that he eat well, to strengthen him for what awaited him. At the end, the reader concluded by saying that Jennia and her son had perished in Auschwitz. I felt then—perhaps not only I—all at once, that the thin bandage that separates our "here" in Israel from the "there" of the Holocaust had suddenly been ripped off.

True, the Pope did not ask for the Jewish people's forgiveness, and did not apologize for the Church's deeds during the Holocaust. Perhaps he refrained from doing so for internal Church political reasons, but to my mind it was just as well.

Think of the outcome had he apologized. Hundreds of millions of Christian believers would have felt that the Pope had absolved them forever of any personal obligation to face up to the Holocaust.

I don't belong to those who believe that the Holocaust was a specifically Jewish event. As I see it, all civilized, fair-minded persons must ask themselves serious questions about the Holocaust and what permitted it to take place.

These are not Jewish questions. They are universal questions about the relations between human beings, about attitudes to the foreign, the different, and the weak. They are questions about the human soul that can so easily be made to stop speaking as "I" and to begin roaring about "we." They are questions about attitudes to force, about the way a person can preserve his humanity in the face of an arbitrary power that seeks to obliterate him, and about the greatest courage of all—the courage to do a kindness to the oppressed, when it is so easy to collaborate with evil.

It is good that the Pope did not ask for forgiveness. No one can ask for forgiveness for the Holocaust in the name of others, and no person may forgive in the name of the victims. The Pope's presence in Yad Vashem, within the most profound dimension of Jewish suffering, like the deeds of human kindness that he, as a human being, performed during the war, are more eloquent than any official declaration.

It is impossible to sum up what happened in the Holocaust in one sentence, or in one gesture, as important as that gesture might be. What happened there will remain forever mute, like a mouth wide open to scream. Something of that cry is present in the silent, missing line at the end of the poem by Dan Pagis, "Scrawled in Pencil in a Sealed Boxcar":

*Here in this transport*
*Am I Eve*
*With my son Abel*
*If you see my oldest son*
*Cain son of Adam*
*Tell him that I*

**DAY FOUR: SERVICE AT THE MOUNT OF BEATITUDES**

Yesterday, for three hours, faith and myth united concretely with the landscape in which events happened, with the names that became the building blocks of Western civilization.

More than anything else, you could perceive, in the faces of the people sitting in wheelchairs, the sense that this was a once-in-a-lifetime event. You could feel—and identify with all your heart—the magnitude of the hope and the faith here, in this place, where miracles happened.

And I, the Jew that I am, watched the ceremony, and I thought that this was the first time that most of the Jews in Israel had seen a Catholic prayer ritual. I know this may seem strange to anyone who has grown up and lived in a Christian country, or anyone accustomed to thinking of the Jews as a tiny minority, but this is the reality in Israel, and if you think about the history of relations between Jews and Christians, maybe you will be able to understand the Jewish aversion to everything having to do with Christianity and with Christian religious institutions.

Jewish pupils in the Israeli school system know almost nothing about Jesus or Christianity. They study about the Christians, generally, in the context of their persecution of the Jews.

I can testify—with some embarrassment—that I never met a single Christian person before I was ten years old (yes, yes, in little, provincial Jerusalem of the 1960s) and that what I knew about Christians came from scary stories about their cruelty toward Jews.

I'm relating this because the service yesterday at Corazin, the Mount of the Beatitudes, was a unique opportunity for millions of Israelis to shed some of these inborn stereotypes and to see—perhaps for the first time—Christianity's other face. Jewish Israelis could now discover the humane, socially conscious, peace- and justice-seeking elements in the teachings of the man of Nazareth. Moreover, they could suddenly be close to a Christian religious ceremony without the trepidation and fear that have, for two thousand years, reverberated almost uncontrollably in the hearts of so many Jews, like a survival reflex.

But there is another aspect, a mirror image of the important change that this visit is generating. It has to do with the way the land of Israel, and the Jew, now appear to believing Catholics.

Another personal story: Some years ago I was traveling in Portugal. One night I arrived in a village in the north and lodged in a small family hotel. I wanted to call home. The hotel proprietress volunteered to connect me with the telephone exchange. She asked me where I wanted to call, and I told her "Jerusalem." She gave me a strange look and began to laugh. "That can't be," she said. "You can't dial Jerusalem." When I asked why, she said quite simply, "Because Jerusalem is in heaven."

But when John Paul II is in Israel, all his millions of believers, in all corners of the world, meet Israel. Not only the Holy Land, but the real, quotidian Israel, in which there are flesh-and-blood Jews who are in no way just an abstract symbol of anything.

Because that, perhaps, is the Jewish people's great tragedy—throughout the generations others, the Christians in particular, viewed them as a symbol, as an allegory or metaphor for something else, as an exceptional entity, possessing powers beyond nature, or below it, as the Nazis put it in their definition of the Jews as *Untermensch*.

For thousands of years the Jew was set apart, exiled from reality. From the familiar. His concreteness and humanity were confiscated through the most subtle means of demonization. The wandering Jew, the eternal Jew, Judas Iscariot, the poisoner of wells, the elders of Zion, and hundreds of other Satanic and grotesque images percolated into folklore, religion, language, literature, even science. Perhaps as a result, the Jews took comfort in a no less dangerous faith, that of self-idealization, regarding themselves as a chosen people, a people set apart.

The State of Israel today is an attempt by Jews to live a life that is not ideal, not demonic. To live real life itself. The normal life of a people living in its country, on its land, raising its children, defending itself with its own strength, and trying, at last, to find a way to conduct normal relations with its neighbors.

The Pope now sees this new, fragile normality, and so do the thousands of pilgrims who came with him, and his billion believers, and all those who watch his journey on television. I say this without forgetting all the difficult problems that Israel has become entangled in during these many decades. Also, without forgetting the injustice that it still inflicts on others. But through the Pope's private eyes, and through the eyes of the generations that he represents, it seems to me that we can also make out the new and growing desire of the Jewish people to be, finally, part of the world, not just part of a story, of a myth, of a heavenly Jerusalem.

## DAY FIVE: MASS IN NAZARETH

The world held its breath for a minute. A man, old and sick, knelt and communed with his God. In the midst of the worldwide media tumult, in the heart of the almost Woodstock-like euphoria that has overcome nearly everyone who has a part in the visit, a single man closed his eyes and was entirely alone. In this journey of his, John Paul II has succeeded in excising layers of spiritual, political, and religious cataract from many things he has touched. Yesterday, and not for the first time, it was possible to appreciate for a moment the secret of this man's personal charisma, even in his dealings with the media.

Maybe it is his appearance. Anyone can immediately empathize with his stooped back, the tremor in his hands, his slow movements, his physical agonies. Maybe it's because of the different, so untelegenic tempo of his movements, of his steps, of his reticent gaze, watching the commotion surrounding him like someone gazing at life from elsewhere, from some other dimension. Perhaps it is because of his rare ability to guard his privacy—even his intimacy—in the middle of the hue and cry surrounding him. Either way, he forces the media to cast aside their conventions about how they relate to a subject. When we see his image on the television screen, we intuit simultaneously his symbolic, ceremonial figure, as well as the individual man on whom we can project our sensibilities and deepest wishes, perhaps even better than on that symbol, the official figure. Here is food for thought: It's precisely those qualities that make the man Karol Wojtyla so untelegenic by the merciless normal criteria that make him so human and moving, a real media megastar.

A similar paradox, deceptive and much more problematic, has to do with the personal qualities of this man, and of the religious establishment he represents.

When he knelt, we forgot for a moment what surrounded him: a huge church building, impressive in its beauty, but grandiose, ostentatious, built at a cost of millions of dollars. To an outsider, a nonreligious one, the church in Nazareth looks like a metaphor for spiritual coagulation, a kind of elephantiasis of the private faith between man and his God. The church seems to be completely foreign to the spirit of simplicity and humility, and to the modesty of Jesus himself.

And for a moment we also forgot that this Pope vehemently opposes birth control, and in so doing prevents progress in the status of women and social development in Third World countries. Still, he knelt in the Church of the Annunciation in Nazareth, in the place where, according to the Catholic faith, Mary received the announcement of her pregnancy. And at that moment I felt how all this exaggerated magnificence, all the flab of this overly wealthy, overly powerful, materialistic, bureaucratic, conservative establishment vanished for a single moment, and withdrew to its real roots, to the sensibility that created it. It harked back to an era when religious faith—and not just Christian faith—was a matter of private dialogue between man and his Creator, without trying to impose itself, generating rivers of blood, on other people. Suddenly there was just one elderly man, his body anguished, and he knew that all the magnificence and grandeur around him did not protect him from pain, and from the most profound human fear. Even the most secular of eyes, eyes which cannot and do not want to find comfort in any religious faith, could then see the kernel of religious emotion, and mourn for what has happened to this authentic sentiment over the course of thousands of years.

## DAY SIX: IN JERUSALEM

Jerusalem is a hard city. Every one of its inhabitants knows it. History is so dense here that it sometimes seems as if the city turns you, despite yourself, into a player on a giant stage, with a single huge but hidden eye watching you.

Perhaps that's why everything in it is overstated, larger than life. Every twinge turns immediately into the agonies of the Son of God; every soccer victory augurs the Messiah's arrival. Every love affair resonates with the love of David and Bathsheba. It's hardly surprising, then, that each year a hundred or so tourists lose their mind in the city. This strange, unique phenomenon even has an official diagnosis: the Jerusalem Syndrome.

Yes, it is hard to live a normal, inconsequential life here. "Jerusalem, a port on the shores of the eternal," the Jerusalem poet Yehuda Amichai wrote. And eternity, what can I tell you, is a pain. The people, even the most common people, are full of a strange self-importance, inflated with the glory of the past. They are quick to be insulted, always feeling as if they are the representatives of something awesome. There's too much holiness in the air. I remember, from my childhood, a tiny backyard on one of the city's side streets where a huge graffiti summed up the nature of this city: HOLY SITE—NO PISSING ALLOWED!

Four thousand years of history, of civilization, of the different cultures that were created here and passed through here. The cradle of Jewish and Christian thought, the center of the three great monotheistic religions. So much wisdom, life experience, knowledge of human suffering and weakness have collected here, and what have we all really learned? Have we—Jews, Christians, and Muslims—really succeeded in being better people, more tolerant of our neighbors?

John Paul II came to this city today. In many ways, the visit here was perhaps the climax of his journey, yet it was the least uplifting day. The streets were nearly empty, and there was tension in the air. Politics brushed aside human warmth.

But this does not detract from the day's historic events: the visit to the mosques on the Temple Mount, the visit to the Western Wall. Perhaps you need to be Jewish to understand the significance of the moment: *The Pope at the Western Wall.* Even this phrase sounds like an oxymoron.

Excuse me if I speak for a moment as a resident of Jerusalem (that is, with all that history on my shoulders). The Western Wall stands above all other Jewish national or religious symbols; it is the most important monument to the Jewish people's continuity. Paradoxically, the fact that it is not whole, that it is but a remnant of the Temple that was destroyed, has made it into what it is in the consciousness of every Jew in the world. Jews have prayed in its direction three times a day, a depiction of the wall hung in the home of nearly every Jew in the Diaspora, and scraps of paper bearing their most intimate requests of God were interred in the fissures among its large stones.

The Pope's visit here today testifies, principally, to Judaism's enormous life force. This tiny nation, numbering twelve million people—about equal to the number of inhabitants of Cairo or London—has succeeded, over four thousand years, in preserving a culture, language, and identity, despite countless attempts to destroy all these. It also has succeeded in instilling, in the hearts of its most bitter enemies—the Church in the past, the Arab states today—the understanding that it must be reckoned with. Acknowledged not only for its existence, but also for the importance of its contribution to mankind.

But that's not all. The Pope, in coming here, in his entire visit, taught us that something else is possible. That even religious establishments, those dogmatic institutions, may grow through openness to and curiosity about other religions. It is hardly credible that, in the third millennium, religions will continue to be nurtured by the hatred of the other. On the contrary, they must begin to carry out their moral and humane precepts. The time has come for a revision of relations between religions and nations.

That, I think, is the essence of the Pope's visit in Israel.

Over the course of six days, John Paul II succeeded in capturing the hearts of Jews, Arabs, and Christians. The most surprising effect he had was on the Jews. It had to do with his personal history from the time of World War II, and with his positions toward the Jewish people, but it was also a result of his unique personality. He captured the hearts of Israelis in a way that few foreign leaders have ever done before. A cabdriver from Tiberias expressed this sentiment best: "What a sweet guy that Pope is. If you ask me, he's really a Jew!" (And I'm sure that the Pope would appreciate the compliment.)

For six days we followed him into the forge of our identity, Jews, Arabs, and Christians, Israelis and Palestinians. We were with him in places where our wounds are still bleeding. But somehow, in a wonderful way that is new to us, his visit made us consider how different and better our lives here could be if we stopped seeing the Other as an existential threat. If we began, for a change, to take joy in the variety of cultural and human richness that this country, and the entire region, offers.

True, the war over geopolitical issues did not really cease during his visit, yet this heavyset man, whose face is both elderly and childlike, passed through at his slow, meditative gait, and with simple gestures made connections between churches, mosques, and the Western Wall. He connected the suffering of the Palestinians in the refugee camps with the most profound fears of the Israelis. He linked the great miracles of ancient days with the little miracles of our daily lives.

I do not know what of all this will remain in our region after he returns to his own land. It's reasonable to assume that, in the days to come, if the negotiations between Israel and Syria and the Palestinians resume, the sides will again take more extreme positions, sparking hostility anew.

But for one week a different wind blew here; there was a sense of reconciliation. For a moment we tasted the possibility of a different kind of life, free of hatred and the exhausting need to always be an enemy. For this small miracle I, a nonreligious Jew, say to John Paul II: Thank you.

# Despite It All

JULY 2000

*Two weeks of marathon negotiations in Camp David between Barak and Arafat and their teams came to a disappointing finish at the end of July 2000. Despite President Clinton's continuous efforts to force both sides to make compromises and to reach a much-needed agreement, they blamed each other—as they continue to do to this day—for the failure of this crucial summit. Insider reports claimed that the major disagreements were over the status of Jerusalem and the Palestinian "right of return." The personalities of the Israeli and Palestinian leaders also seem to have contributed to the difficulties in the negotiations.*

## I

Yesterday was a heartbreaking day for all those who hoped that the Israeli and Palestinian people had finally comprehended that if they cannot live together, they cannot live at all. The cheers of the extremists of both nations demonstrated, more than anything else, the fearsome perversion that we have become so accustomed to: the prospect of war delights many on both sides much more than does the possibility of peace.

In keeping with his character, Ehud Barak arrived at the summit confident, audacious, and truly wanting to end the conflict forever. Perhaps from the start there was not much likelihood that such an ambitious program would succeed, but on the other hand, after a century of antagonism, all the problems are already known, all the obstacles are familiar, so why not launch a full-scale charge toward peace with the same force and determination we have used charging on the battlefield?

Indeed, the innovation in these talks—and the source of hope for the future—was that the two sides were able, for the first time, to touch the conflict's raw nerves—the question of the refugees, the Palestinians' right of return, the settlements, and the status of Jerusalem.

Touching these nerves led, of course, to the predictable reflex—the body politic instantly jerked and tensed, both people's muscles cramped up, and religious adrenaline flowed into the national bloodstreams.

Numerous Israelis and Palestinians immediately enlisted in the campaign to shore up defenses against the threat of compromise. Both sides promulgated religious rulings, signed by rabbis and Muslim muftis, declaring that there could be no territorial compromise in the land of our forefathers. The Palestinians went even further and announced that any leader who agreed to such a compromise, especially on holy Jerusalem, al-Quds, would be denounced as a traitor—his fate a bullet in the head. The army and the police, in Israel and the Palestinian Authority, were put on alert, and their commanders issued threatening warnings. Barak's government was left with almost no ministers who supported his strange eagerness to make peace; and Arafat's ministers tried to outdo each other with warnings against making any concession. And the result?

The two peoples proved once again that they are still not

capable of living together, yet neither are they able to disconnect from each other. They did not have the fortitude to take the final step, the one that would have led to a real metamorphosis in their relations. Even after the extraordinary American effort at mediation, they remained in a clinch, strangling each other in a double nelson, victims of the cowardly and fanatic way of thinking that so many years of hatred have created. The maps that tried to trace new borders, convoluted and peppered with enclaves, demonstrated to all the impossible snarl of the current situation, resembling a divorce agreement between a husband and wife who must continue to live out their lives in the same apartment, and sometimes even in the same bed.

## II

We do not know yet what actually happened in the negotiating rooms, who conceded and who refused to concede. We have the exceptional testimony of President Clinton himself, according to which Barak was more flexible and more daring. But the Palestinians will, of course, claim the opposite.

Despite the reservations the Israeli left has about Ehud Barak's somewhat military vision of peace, and about his attitude toward the Palestinians during the negotiations, it should be stated unequivocally that no previous Israeli leader has been so determined and decisive in seeking to make peace, and so bold in the concessions he was offering to achieve it. But did Barak really go the whole possible distance? Did he really, as he claimed, "turn over every stone" in his efforts to compromise? On the other hand, had he dared turn over even one more "sacred" stone—for example, by ceding the Palestinians sovereignty over a significant part of

East Jerusalem—would he have been able to win the Israeli people's approval of the agreement in the referendum he promised? Is Israeli society ready for such a move?

Another question nagging all those who wanted this summit to succeed: Did Barak have a real partner at Camp David for his far-reaching moves? True, there is no symmetry between the concessions other two sides can make. Israel holds almost all the cards, while the Palestinians have more restricted options. Nevertheless, there is no escaping the sense that Arafat was the less bold, less creative, and more stubborn of the two leaders. Even one who has great sympathy for the long suffering and the impossible position of the Palestinians cannot avoid the impression that Arafat was at fault this time in his analysis of the situation, as he has been more than once in the past.

Had Arafat shown any flexibility at all on the question of Jerusalem, he might have succeeded in getting Barak to take even larger strides, in the end breaking through the psychological snare that now paralyzes the entire process. Had Arafat been freer of the pressures exerted by the extremists among his people, and of the pressure of other Arab leaders, perhaps he would have avoided the scenario that now casts its shadow over many in Israel—the possibility that the extremists on the right will gain power and Benjamin Netanyahu returns to the political arena. If such developments occur, it will be almost impossible to achieve peace in the future.

But perhaps what is required is superhuman courage of a kind that the two leaders are not yet ready for. This they must have in order to dare change anything fundamental in their attitudes toward Jerusalem.

I wonder whether anyone who is not part of the local drama, and who observes it only from outside, can really appreciate the force of the emotions, the yearnings, and the compulsions that the old city of Jerusalem rouses in those who live in or around it. This area, hardly half a mile square, is so charged with history, myth, memory, wars, and the profound essence of so many cultures and of the three major religions that it has become a kind of black hole of incredibly dense mass that threatens to suck the whole region into it.

Despite this, Ehud Barak became the first Israeli leader to agree to put Jerusalem on the negotiating table. Barak did this, and Arafat was not prepared, or able, to make *any* move toward him. Barak withstood enormous pressure from his own people, yet he did not rule out flexibility or a re-examination of ossified historical positions. Arafat turned him away with a categorical refusal. In this, Arafat bears greater responsibility for the summit's failure.

But the minute the Jerusalem question was made a subject of negotiation, many Israelis dared come out of the closet and admit that Israel's claim of the "sanctity of united Jerusalem" is but an empty slogan. Jerusalem has never been united. Two hostile nations live within it. They maintain largely separate social and government institutions. Suddenly, in the past week, many Israelis discovered the huge gap between the authentic, real core of historical and religious Jerusalem, about which our forefathers dreamed throughout thousands of years of exile, and real-life Jerusalem. The latter contains twenty-six Palestinian villages that Israeli governments annexed to the city for political reasons. They then began swearing in its name and endowing it with the sanctity of biblical Zion.

This past week I visited some of those villages, together with Minister of Justice Yossi Beilin. I sought to discover whether they create any sort of religious frisson in me. Does any sort of national, historic shiver run through me that would testify to my connection with these places? When my grandfather in Warsaw closed his eyes and directed his heart to Jerusalem, did his soul long for the Palestinian village of Wallageh? Was it for the Qalandia refugee camp that the twelfth-century Jewish poet Yehuda Halevy yearned from distant Spain: "The savor of your soil delights my mouth like honey"?

I felt nothing. I discovered what I had long known: the boundaries of Jewish-Israeli identity actually need much less Jerusalem than what the municipal boundaries contain. The question is only whether Israel will—as its right-wingers demand—put up its future as collateral in order to battle for such an illusory identification with this manipulative Jerusalem, or whether Israelis can now define for themselves what their *true* spiritual, security, and religious interests are—and strive for them alone.

Now, after the acute despair of last night, it is clearer than ever that the peace process must go on, because if it stops for even a moment, despair and extremists will take control. The process will continue on its agonizing, bumpy way, requiring all of us to ask the most difficult questions of ourselves, about our identity, our faith, and our courage or cowardice. I hope that this is not just my own dream: I believe that there will be flexibility on the question of Jerusalem, on both sides. When the moment comes—may we not need another round of bloodshed before it does—both sides will realize that not only Jerusalem is holy; the lives of the people who live there are no less holy.

## Boy Killed in Gaza

OCTOBER 2000

*The tragic killing of a twelve-year-old Palestinian boy on September 30, 2000, was televised and broadcast live around the world. Muhammad al-Durrah, who died in his wounded father's arms, became an instant international symbol of the Palestinian uprising. To this day, neither the Palestinian Authority nor the Israeli Army has accepted responsibility for the death of the child in the crossfire between them.*

Everyone who lives in this disaster area—the Middle East—has seen many horrific sights. But these pictures, the pictures of Muhammad al-Durrah's death, are among the most harrowing ever seen here. They signify that even if we eventually have peace in the end, it may arrive too late.

Because war and violence have blinded our eyes, and have turned some of us into killers, and many others of us into tacit collaborators with murderers.

Of course, there is still no way of knowing who shot him, Israelis or Palestinians. In the madness that rages here, anything is possible. But there can be no absolution for such an act—for the execution of a twelve-year-old boy. When I hear Israeli Army officers explaining that the father shouldn't have taken his son to a riot zone, I feel nauseated.

For more than one hundred years we, Israelis and Palestinians, have been giving birth to children in battlefields, bullets shrieking past us. Yet another generation and another generation are thrown into the fire immediately at birth. Our parents did this to us, and we are doing it to our children. Fathers cannot defend their sons, but it also seems that they do not have the strength to rise above this fate for their families, to change this verdict. As if all of us here, Palestinians and Israelis, are doomed to be either murderers or victims.

As if we no longer have any other way.

In the meantime, for the last year and a half, Barak and Arafat have not stopped talking about the need to make peace, *for the sake of the children*. But they are apparently speaking of some abstract peace, and of figurative children.

A twelve-year-old boy now lies between them, a boy with a name and a face, a face contorted with fear. A very tangible dead boy.

Were Barak and Arafat braver, really brave, this boy might still be alive. Now, even if they reach an agreement in the end, we will carry Muhammad al-Durrah's face in our minds like a curse.

Who knows how many more innocent people will die in the days to come, until the two sides understand that the look that was in the eyes of that boy before he died will be the look we all have if we continue to sit passively, easy prey for violence.

## Letter to a Palestinian Friend

OCTOBER 2000

*The second Intifada broke out after the failure of the negotiations between Israel and the Palestinians at Camp David. It was instigated by a visit of opposition leader Ariel Sharon to the Temple Mount (al-Haram al-Sharif) in the old city of Jerusalem, on September 28, 2000. Palestinians regarded the visit to the site, sacred to both Muslims and Jews, as a provocation, and the riots that erupted the next day resulted in many deaths. The wave of violence that spread throughout the West Bank and Gaza was met with overwhelming force by Israeli security.*

*On October 12, 2000, two Israeli reservists lost their way near Ramallah and were stopped by the Palestinian police. An angry Palestinian mob invaded the police station and brutally stabbed the Israelis to death, then mutilated their bodies. Shocking film footage of the murders convinced many Israelis that there was no hope of achieving a negotiated peace with the Palestinians.*

Dear B.,

First, I hope you are well, and that no one in your family has been hurt in the events of these last weeks.

I was thinking how strange—and sad—it is that we have not spoken on the phone since the disturbances began. Up until then, after any event that took place during the peace process, joyous or violent, we always spoke, or even met (though the meetings were rarer). And now—absolute silence. Perhaps because we are both in shock, shock that paralyzes our ability to respond and our strength to continue to believe. Being in shock, we might both be thinking at this moment that we may have erred. Maybe we only imagined that we saw the incipience of hope in both our peoples. Maybe the whole concept of peace was the naïve illusion of a few bleeding hearts that were weary of war and oblivious to the volcano of primal instincts and hatred churning under their feet.

Or perhaps we don't dare call each other because somewhere, in your heart also, I'm sure, nestles the fear that the friend, the Other, has already despaired completely of conciliation. Maybe even he, moderate and judicious, has finally been inundated by the wave of hatred that has broken over all of us now.

But no. I don't believe that this is what happened to you. We've known each other for eight years, talked about literature and politics, about life, about our children. It feels strange to me to address you in this way, publicly, and even now, at the opening of this letter, I feel a slight change in my normal manner of speaking to you. Over the years we have freed ourselves from the natural tendency of all Israelis and Palestinians who engage in dialogue to turn themselves into representatives of their people. But at this time, the new situation threatens to relegate us to that position, whether we like it or not.

You know, when I watch the television broadcasts, I always try to watch them through your eyes. I see a Palestinian throng storming an Israeli Army position and I try to single out an individual face, which might be the face of one of your children. I know that you don't approve of this kind of demonstration, that it is foreign to your character, as one who opposes all forms of violence. But perhaps, under these new circumstances, it is hard to control a teenage boy who was but a toddler at the time of the first Intifada. Perhaps he has grown up on the proud, heroic stories of the teenage boys of that time and now longs to take part in his people's resolute, violent struggle for independence. I gaze at the photographs, seeing how the hands are raised, holding stones; how the faces are contorted with hatred. I see the Israeli soldiers taking aim and shooting, and think of my own son, who will soon enlist in the army. Will his face and body also quickly adjust to those attitudes of war and hatred? I look, and suddenly all of them, our children and your children, have the same faces and the same gestures, and it is so clear the extent to which the long conflict has succeeded in claiming them for itself, all of them. All look to me like toy soldiers, lacking individual volition, marionettes manipulated by politicians and army commanders on both sides.

And I try to think of what you are experiencing, you with your sober, accommodating views, within a society that from the outside looks to me as if it is ablaze with a fire for revenge. You are within a nation that is now roaring at me, at least on the television screen, with a single voice, without nuances. But perhaps I am mistaken. Maybe you, and other common friends of ours, are making their voices heard. Maybe it's the media—ours and yours and the world's—that chooses to show only the harshest, most extreme scenes and stir up our feelings against each other. But even if the media is guilty, as we always claim in Israel, how is it possible that I have not heard a single note of sincere Palestinian condemnation of the horrible lynching of the two soldiers in Ramallah—and I mean an explicit condemnation, with no buts and with no "you must understand Palestinian anger."

And are you over there, beyond the present wall of alienation, aware that among us you can still hear, even after all that has happened, voices that insist on questioning whether Israel indeed did *everything* for peace, and what is the real nature of the peace that we imposed on the Palestinians, and whether we did not again fail by viewing reality through our spectacles of bottomless fear, our permanent blind spot? (But, after all, it is an eminently justifiable fear, a voice shouts within me, because in the face of all that we have seen, it is all so rational to fear!) I know that it is impossible to compare the limitations that you are subject to, to the freedom of expression that I have here, in Israel. The worst thing that can happen to me if I express an opinion that is far off the consensus is that someone will write a venomous article against me. But you might be physically harmed. But I so much want to hear, at this hour, in a private conversation, what you are thinking now.

If it's at all possible to think now as the riots rage outside, and inside. All day—arguments. I drive my car and argue with myself. Friends testify that even in bed, with their spouses, they talk almost solely about politics. The human spirit cringes. I also realize that for every argument I make, I have an incontrovertible counterargument. The situation is so complex and unavoidable that even opinions I always opposed suddenly bear an ominous attraction. People accost me angrily in the street. Everything you believed in was just a dream, they say. You can't make peace with the Palestinians. How can you believe Arafat, who has already signed four agreements in which he committed himself to refrain from the use of violence? How can you believe beasts like those who lynched the soldiers? What a horrible, criminal blunder it was to give the Palestinians weapons, with which they are now shooting and killing us.

I don't know how it is with you, but here close friends, and even relatives, who always believed in peace, and hoped that most of the Palestinians were undergoing a similar process, now feel truly brokenhearted and betrayed. What was the point of offering Arafat so much, of compromising even on Jerusalem, when he encourages such violence, when there is no certainty that he can control his people, and when the schools and mosques of the Palestinian Authority continue to teach and preach the destruction of Israel?

And beyond that, Israelis say today—you can hear it everywhere—even if we give the Palestinians everything, all the territories, and evacuate the settlements and even hand over all of East Jerusalem—the following day they'll want the rest of Jerusalem, and Haifa and Jaffa. They'll always find a new pretext for violence, for nurturing their hatred and their yearning to throw us into the sea. I have my own answers to those questions, nowadays somewhat more hesitant. I still believe there's truth in these answers, but I feel how weak this reasoning is, in light of the fire and the fury of hatred.

Suddenly, in an impulse of despair, out of isolation, and in protest of the situation that prevents me from doing something so simple and natural, I call you.

You recognize my voice at once, and I hear your relief. We speak for a long time. Your family is unharmed, but the little boy next door was killed. I tell you that bullets were fired tonight on the Jerusalem neighborhood where my brother lives. We both still observe a kind of symmetry, a balance in our reporting, which of course balances nothing, nor does it comfort; despite it all, we are still representatives. You sound agitated and beyond hope—I have never heard you sound this way. It is a nightmare, you say, never has the situation been as awful, and there is no way of knowing how it will end. You blame Israel. The way it dragged out the negotiations for years, far beyond what was agreed on at Oslo. You speak of the impossibility of reaching peace without evacuating the settlements. About how Israel humiliated the Palestinians in the negotiations, and then went so far as to demand that they consider intra-Israeli political problems, while completely ignoring Arafat's shaky position. Israel tried to impose peace on him under conditions that no Palestinian, even the most moderate, would accept.

I agree with you that the way Israel conducted the peace process was faulty, aggressive, hostage to profound Israeli fears, and unable to empathize with the Palestinian point of view. For years I've thought that the peace agreement itself, as it was engineered in Oslo, was the product of brusque Israeli dictation, and that the reality it was meant to create was not going to ensure neighborly relations. Despite that, I say, look at the change that has taken place in Israel with regard to peace since the Oslo process began, especially in the past year, under Barak's administration. Can you deny the man's courage, his willingness—which astounded and incensed many Israelis—to hand over most of the occupied territories to you, and to give up parts of Jerusalem, the innermost heart of the Jewish people? Don't you know, as I do, that a generation's worth of years will pass before there is another Israeli leader who is both so courageous and able to retain the confidence of the Israeli people in his defense policy? And if you miss this opportunity, you'll find yourselves facing Sharon (and we, too—I think to myself—we, too, will find ourselves in that dangerous position).

You are familiar with my arguments and respond to them with your arguments, which are familiar to me. It is as if both of us have to quote them repeatedly, are trapped within them, and feel that our positions never completely capture the whole dilemma. There's always that humiliating sensation that we—the Israeli and the Palestinian—are nothing but a pair of actors sentenced to acting on stage, generation after generation, a grotesque and bloody tragedy whose denouement no one can write, a scene that would offer a hope of relief, of the lifting of the curse.

What frightens me, you say, is that the debate now is not only between governments, or between our armies and police, but between the peoples, the civilians. And the worst is that after Sharon's visit to the Temple Mount, it has once more become a feral, tribal, and religious battle.

It seems to me that the situation deteriorated not with Sharon's visit to the Temple Mount, which was, in and of itself, provocative and malicious, but rather when Arafat announced three months ago at Camp David that he could not sign a compromise agreement on Jerusalem. He represents, he said then, not only five million Palestinians but also the world's billion Muslims. At that moment, to my mind, the possibility of a solution eluded us, and it turned into a religious conflict. You and I know that religious fanaticism, whether Jewish or Muslim, is your and my real enemy. Neither you nor I can live our lives as we desire under an extremist religious regime. In the end, the relevant borders for most Israelis and Palestinians are not only those between the two people, for all their importance, but those between the moderates and extremists on both sides. That should be one of our major motives for reaching a compromise, at almost any price, in order to weaken the religious forces that are growing so strong now.

But we cannot accept the solutions you are offering us, you say—there can be no peace with the settlements, there can be no peace when what we finally get, after such a long struggle, is a tiny state without control of our water sources and most of our territory, a state crosscut by hundreds of Israeli roads and roadblocks. There can be no peace when every time I open my blinds in the morning I see the settlement on the mountaintop that looms over me. Do you know that the settlers call me every night and demand that I leave my city? They, who only twenty years ago settled here by force.

It won't be a just peace, I admit, but I hope that as a first step it will be a good-enough peace. We can't hope for more than that in the meantime, but maybe afterward, many years from now, when animosity has diminished, when a normal fabric of life has been established, perhaps even trust renewed . . .

I want you to know, you say out of context, how sad and shocked I was by the lynching of the Israeli soldiers. It is horrifying. I blame the Palestinian police, because no matter how the Israelis got there, from the minute unarmed people are under your protection, you must safeguard them. No, such an atrocity simply must not be allowed to happen. Even in such a brutal struggle we must retain our humanity.

I ask if there are others who think as you do, and you say that the great majority of Palestinians were appalled by the incident. I have trouble believing you. The sight of the faces of the murderers and their cries of carnage are still so vivid in my memory. The hands proudly raised aloft, soaked in the blood of the murdered men. I then recall a conversation we had not long ago in a Jerusalem café, before the world turned over on all of us. There we concurred that the Oslo agreement had been possible because the two leaders, Rabin and Arafat, had finally realized, after years of holding to a militant, aggressive worldview, that the conflict was seeping into the innermost tissues of their peoples, infecting them with violence and brutality, and decomposing them from within.

And you remind me that we said one more thing on that day. We had no illusions about this—we knew that this peace process would be a bitter one. That it would be full of successive acts of enmity and violence on both sides, acts that time after time would move Israelis and Palestinians to cry out in rage, each in turn, Look how impossible it is to believe them! Look what a mistake we made when we made sacrifices to them! We'll never, never live in peace side by side!

And so it was.

But never to this extent.

You interrupt the conversation for a moment, telling your wife that you forgot a dish in the oven. I hear your children laughing in the background. Your home. Things television doesn't show.

Afterward you say, Look, you and I, we represent two overly emotional peoples. For that reason, so much depends on how our leaders lead us. For example, you say, I think that we Palestinians have to change the way we fight. I don't believe it's good to send children to throw stones, nor adults either. We need to find a nonviolent mode of struggle, a peaceful struggle, because the loss of life is terrible. But also because our behavior threatens you, and you respond overaggressively, not willing to listen to us. We need to turn to peaceful demonstrations, you say—maybe that way we can get across to you what we feel. But you, too, must change. You shouldn't exaggerate the situation as if it is a threat to your existence.

You're certainly right about that, I reply. I see that this brief conflict has revealed just how deep our existential fear is. That, perhaps, is the Palestinian tragedy, that you are facing a tough and complicated partner (one convinced it is the meekest, most malleable, most merciful partner there is). You have a partner with a history so difficult that nothing in the universe can give it a real sense of security and strength.

If you were more confident, you say, you wouldn't use such heavy fire against demonstrators. Just think of what massive power you use against us.

"The peace of the brave," I say, quoting Arafat.

Ah, you suddenly sigh. Politicians are ruthless.

Are you managing to get anything done these days? I ask.

How can I? Who can concentrate?

You could at least state publicly the things you tell me.

No, and certainly not as I once could. But I'm sure that most of the Palestinian public thinks as I do. Listen, people here understand that peace is a necessity. Not everyone here is pleased with all that's happening. We have lost more people than you have, but I know that the Israeli sense of loss is just as great. We feel surrounded, under siege, but so do you. We must break free of this despair and this paralysis because, at the end of the day, we are going to have to live here together and we can't kill each other indefinitely. We'll live here together, I say, and in the end we'll also make peace, but it will be a frail peace, always on the verge of being shattered. And underneath there will always be that volcano, and it will erupt again and again. Hundreds of years may pass before we have, if ever, a peace similar to the one between England and France, or between France and Germany. But what am I doing planning the centuries to come, when the question is what to do now, today?

Today we will do nothing, you say. Today both your and our blood is boiling. We have to wait a few days and hope that things will calm down a bit. Afterward we'll decide what we can do.

And so, agreeing that we will speak more frequently, we bid each other farewell.

## Stop Mumbling

NOVEMBER 2000

*The al-Aksa Intifada continued to gain momentum, despite a statement made by Arafat and Barak at an emergency summit in Sharm el-Sheikh, initiated by President Clinton, calling for an end to the violence. Inside Israel, heated demonstrations of Arab Israelis in support of the Palestinians resulted in the killing of thirteen demonstrators—all Israeli citizens. An inquiry committee was later established to investigate the Israeli police's excessive use of force. The Israeli public was appalled at the sights of Palestinian violence in Israel and in the occupied territories. Many members of the Israeli left found themselves angry and disappointed with the Palestinian leadership, which seemed to have completely abandoned the path of political negotiations. The "confused left" later contributed, reluctantly but without question, to the rise of a new, strong leader—Ariel Sharon.*

It is hard to believe that very many Israelis will be willing to listen to the Palestinians' claims today, especially when they are accompanied by cruel and bloodcurdling acts of terror. Still, anyone who seeks a solution, who is not willing to be a passive victim of those who sow death and hatred all around us, must listen.

Those who talk today with Palestinians in key positions, officials of the Palestinian Authority and intellectuals, must admit that there is justice in their claims. A look at the map of Palestine that the Oslo process was to create reveals why the Palestinians felt trifled with. They realized that, after a bloody struggle, they would not be granted a real state, but rather a bunch of spots of national identity, surrounded and sliced by the ongoing presence of the Israeli occupier. This, and other, no less harsh claims, means that any defense of the Israeli position requires quite a bit of logical contortion, not to mention moral acrobatics.

When examining the major obstacles that now prevent, as they will in the future, any sort of agreement, you discover the centrality of the issue of the settlements. Is it entirely out of bounds to hope that, after tempers cool a bit, Israel will reopen this subject to discussion? And will it, this time, do so with an understanding that it can no longer impose a solution to this charged issue on the Palestinians? Will Israel recognize that it is in its own manifest interest to endure short-term pain, almost intolerable pain, in order to realize, over generations, its truly essential goals?

The position of official and semiofficial Palestinian spokesmen today is that Israeli settlers who wish to remain in the territories under Palestinian sovereignty will be allowed to do so. The rest must return to Israel. At the same time, the Palestinians accept, without a choice, the possibility that certain settlement blocks will be annexed to Israel, as part of a symmetrical exchange of territory.

It is hard to believe that many Israelis today will agree to trust the goodwill of future Palestinian leaders. They will not entrust their safety to them. But neither do you have to be a great expert to comprehend that no country in the world can accept the existence, deep inside it, of heavily armed and fortified enclaves protected by the soldiers of another country, linked to that other state by dozens of restricted roads. Every rational person must understand that if we do not find a solution to this problem, the situation will quickly deteriorate into a Bosnian one, in which Jewish and Palestinian civilians will be shooting at each other in an endless spiral of blood.

So we have no choice but to say, with no equivocation, what many Israelis have been thinking for years. To achieve a just peace, one that has a real chance of lasting, many settlements will have to be dismantled. Not only the tiny settlements that were intended for evacuation under the Oslo agreement, ones like Ganim, Kadim, and Netzarim, but also others, as large and as established as they may be, whose location is liable to prevent a future agreement. This would include Ofra, Beit El, Elon Moreh, and Kiryat Arba. The same is true of the settlements in the Jordan Valley and on Mt. Hebron, as well as the eastern part of the Gush Etzion block.

We shouldn't feign innocence—the great majority of the settlements were located exactly where they are in order to prevent any chance of a future peace treaty or, to our detriment, to frustrate the creation of a territorially contiguous Palestinian state. Now that this goal has in fact been achieved, complicating the situation to the point of despair, the settlers are proclaiming: See? Under these conditions we can't make peace!

So the moment has come in which all Israelis must ask themselves, honestly, if they really are prepared to be killed for the right of a few thousand settlers to live in armed and alienated enclaves in the midst of an Arab population. Are they prepared to perform reserve duty there, engaging in a Kosovo-style combat against the Palestinians? Are they prepared for their sons and daughters to die defending the settlements?

The constant clashes between Israel and the Palestinians has impelled us more than once to dig ourselves into positions that are clearly very difficult to defend—such as our eighteen-year sojourn in Lebanon. In the end, we are forced to abandon those positions, by the skin of our teeth, after painful bloodletting.

For that reason, this is the time to ask again, as if for the first time, whether the statement "We won the Six-Day War" really requires reaching the conclusion that "we will therefore remain here forever, in the midst of a conquered people." Is this really the only way to take advantage of the great Israeli victory in that war?

For years the peace camp has been mumbling about the necessity to evacuate the settlements. Mumbling, not yelling out loud, both because it recoils at the idea of uprooting families, children who were born there, and because of the fear that such an act will create a national trauma. But we can no longer continue to mumble. Logic requires the uprooting of many settlements that cannot be defended and whose existence will destroy the all-too-fragile chance for peace. In the end, supporters of peace must make this mental switch. The events of the last month, even if they elicit fear and doubt, in fact support such a step, and reveal the great danger inherent in lacking the courage to take this decision.

## An Invitation to Dialogue: Response to a Palestinian Open Letter

NOVEMBER 2000

*In early November 2000, Palestinian intellectuals published in the major Israeli newspapers an urgent letter to the Israeli public. They offered several basic principles that should be fulfilled in order to renew the peace process and end the violence: namely, an end to the Israeli occupation, acceptance of Jerusalem as the capital of both states, and Israeli recognition of its responsibility for the creation of the Palestinian refugee problem. "Peace and co-existence will not be accomplished by imposing an unjust settlement that goes against the will of the people. This land is destined to be the home of our two peoples . . . It is our hope that, out of the tragedies of recent weeks, a new and fair vision of peace can emerge between the two peoples."*

*The author's reply to the Palestinian appeal was published in Arabic in the Palestinian newspaper* al-Ayyam *on November 18, 2000.*

Sirs and Madams:

A week ago, 121 Palestinian academics and public activists published an open letter to the Israeli public. As a member of that public, I would like to respond.

Before I address the substance of what you wrote, I would like to state that the publication of a letter in the Israeli press is of great importance. In these times, each side is hearing only gunshots and belligerent rhetoric, and many have despaired of any rational dialogue. So I would like to thank you for having opened the door to a conversation of a different type, without which we will not reach a solution.

As an Israeli who seeks peace, I agree with no small number of the positions presented in your appeal. This applies both to your description of the harsh reality that prevailed in the occupied territories under the façade of the Oslo Accords and to the pointlessness of a peace agreement that reflects, more than anything else, Israel's military superiority. Similarly, most of the "broad principles" you proposed seem to me to be a possible basis for a future agreement.

However, as an Israeli who seeks peace, what I find missing from your open letter is a statement that such an agreement will constitute the end of all claims on both sides, and that it will contain a recognition of the 1967 borders as the permanent borders between Israel and Palestine. I would have hoped to see such a letter more clearly address the future relations between the two states, a joint war on terror, and a joint campaign against incitement, without which future generations will grow up infected with hatred and racism.

I do not pretend to represent anyone else, but it seems to me that I am not alone in my opinions. A growing number of Israelis recognize that a peace agreement must lead to the establishment of a sovereign and independent Palestinian state. To achieve this, Israel must retreat from almost all the territories it occupied in 1967, evacuating most of the settlements, with consensual border rectifications based on an exchange of territory. Israel's cabinet includes ministers who speak of dividing Jerusalem and turning it into two capitals for the two peoples, together with a compromise on sovereignty over the holy sites. Generous Israeli ideas about the refugee problem are also being proposed today, with the goal of resolving this issue.

I am not trying to claim that these are the opinions of the Israeli majority, but it is also clear to me that they are not those of an insignificant minority.

And that is not something to be taken lightly. The Israeli public now feels threatened, for several reasons. Most Israelis were not at all aware of the depth of Palestinian rage over the way the peace process was conducted. They were taken by surprise by the violence that was directed against them. They had believed that the peace process had brought with it a road map toward reconciliation. Most of the Jewish public in Israel (like most of the Palestinian public) was not familiar with the details of the agreement. Israelis felt that they had already made huge concessions, that they had overcome their anxieties and traumas. And here, right at the finish line, as they saw it, their partners in the process betrayed them, violated a signed agreement, and who knew what more those Palestinians would demand, once they had "received" their independent state.

I am familiar with the Palestinian responses to these claims. I agree with some of them. Yes, the Israelis don't honor agreements. And the Israeli military presence in the occupied territories is violent. There are also the settlements, the areas sealed by the army, and the siege. As well as the brutal military response against stone throwing.

I write these lines and feel the depressing futility of repeating arguments that are so familiar to all of us. What is the point of beating round the bush along the familiar path of recrimination, when hundreds of innocent people, Palestinians and Israelis, are being killed? What is the point, in the current situation, of trying to determine who is guilty, or who started it all? All of us, Israelis and Palestinians, are participants, to one extent or another, in the tragedy that has come upon us. But there's one thing that can't be doubted despite all this fear and confusion: If the leadership on both sides is not truly courageous, Jewish and Palestinian children will continue to kill each other, and we, their parents, will send them to die (and we'll then charge each other with "making use of children").

The al-Aksa Intifada has, with great force, brought Palestinian pain, humiliation, and anger to the surface. The entire world and, within it, many Israelis also, now understand that the Oslo agreements must be reopened and that a new peace agreement, a fairer and bold one, must be drafted. Such an agreement will present difficult challenges to both peoples, perhaps too difficult to bear. Both sides will have to give up concrete and important assets. Both will also have to give up the delusions and illusions that have accounted for their strength and hope and national consciousness.

Every rational person understands that continuing violence, on both sides, is liable to send the region into disaster, into a historical tragedy whose outcome no one can now predict. Neither Israelis nor Palestinians will come out of it well. Maybe only the extremists among both peoples want it. They, in the final analysis, are the true enemies of the majority on both sides.

The Palestinians who signed the open letter to the Israeli public, and the many other Palestinians and Israelis who believe in what I have written here, can still hold discussions among themselves. Of course they are not authorized to conduct negotiations, but at least they have the power to renew the dialogue. Perhaps we will be able to find creative and just solutions at the points where the politicians—for a variety of reasons—are not able to rise above their short-term interests.

As an Israeli who seeks peace, I ask: Can we meet—yes, even in these times—on the border, both the metaphorical and the concrete demarcation, somewhere between Palestine and Israel, say, in a peace tent that we erect there together? Can we present an alternative of any sort to the rampant animosity, hatred, killing, and revenge? Can we halt the mad, violent whirlwind that threatens to sweep up all of us?

Here: this is an invitation to dialogue.

# Point of No Return

JANUARY 2001

*A major point of contention between Palestinians and Israelis continues to be the "right of return" of the Palestinian refugees. About eight hundred thousand people who fled or were expelled from Palestine during the 1948 War of Independence between the newly established state of Israel and four Arab countries were kept by the Arab states in refugee camps in Lebanon, Jordan, the Jordanian West Bank, and the Egyptian-ruled Gaza Strip. After the Six-Day War, when Israel conquered the West Bank and Gaza, the refugees in those territories came under Israeli control. The ongoing dispute over Israel's responsibility for the creation of the refugee problem has not been resolved. The number of Palestinian refugees today is estimated at 5.5 million people around the world.*

The "right of return" has been a central Palestinian demand for the last fifty-two years. Yet only in recent weeks has it penetrated Israeli consciousness as a concrete and threatening possibility. It now looks as if the Palestinian insistence on the "right of return" will lead even the most steadfast of Israeli doves—myself included—to the reluctant and disheartening conclusion that peace cannot be achieved at this time.

Many Israelis live with an inner conflict between their moral and natural desire to repair a decades-old injustice and their profound apprehensions about the "right of return." The prospect of the return of the Palestinian refugees who fled or were expelled from Israel during and after the War of Independence confronts every Jewish Israeli with the most problematic roots of Israel's definition of itself as the Jewish state. The Jewish majority's explicit desire to retain its numerical superiority is one that, when it comes down to it, beats in the hearts of every nation. Every nation wishes to preserve its values and heritage and pass them on to the generations to come; such an aspiration is neither jingoistic nor racist. In the case of the Jewish people, with their tragic history, it is even more comprehensible, although it remains an unresolved discrepancy in the democracy they desire.

In my view, accepting the Palestinian demand would be a dangerous move for Israel as a Jewish state, and as a political entity. Israel must accept its *partial* responsibility for the refugee problem, alongside the Arab countries that created the problem in 1948. Israel must help raise the funds to resettle the refugees, and must allow some refugees to return for purely humanitarian reasons. Likewise, Israel must recognize the refugees' bonds to the places they were torn away from. But there is a great distance between an affinity to a place and the "right to return" there.

The Palestinians have been trying to reassure Israelis by explaining that even if the agreement refers to the "right of return," it will be only a formal right. In practice, they say, "only" a few hundred thousand refugees will resettle inside Israel (where there are today five million Jews and a million Palestinians). I don't understand this distinction. A right is a right, and if a right is granted, it exists in full. Anyone with a sense of responsibility for the generations to come must today consider how, fifty years from now, his great-grandchildren will explain to the great-grandchildren of today's refugees that the "right of return" that Israel recognized was only a theoretical one, a formality.

For decades the Israeli peace camp, together with the Palestinian peace camp, has worked to disseminate the concept of "two states for two peoples." In other words, a Palestinian national state that will live in security and peace alongside the State of Israel, the Jewish national state. Yet the demand for a sweeping "right of return" will lead, in practice, to a situation in which the Palestinians have a national state, Palestine, while Israel becomes, instead of a Jewish state, a Jewish and Palestinian state—in other words, a political entity whose identity will gradually become blurred.

Jewish villages and cities have been built during the last fifty years on the ruins of the villages in which the Palestinian refugees once lived. This is a heartrending fact for the refugees, but changing it would require tearing millions of Jews away from their homes, and to where? Let us not forget that the great majority of these Jews are themselves members of refugee families who fled ancestral homes in Europe and the Islamic world. Will committing yet another injustice bring the two peoples closer to peace?

"What do you mean?" my Palestinian friends ask me when we blow up at each other during arguments, time after time, over this issue. "If Israel accepts the principle of the 'right of return,'" they argue, "and the refugees indeed return, an entirely new reality will be created here, a reality of conciliation and mutual forgiveness, a reality of true peace."

If that could only be true. I desperately want to believe it can. It certainly fits my natural inclinations to dream, as they do, of a peace that will come to be despite the violence around and among us. I long for a world in which all the hate, hurt, and suspicion of the past are nobly set aside. But as one who lives in this deeply divided, extremist, fundamentalist region, I know that a good solution is one that tries—at least in its early stages—to do everything possible to avoid friction between rival populations. It must be a solution that does not impose too difficult a test on our faith in the goodwill of either Jews or Muslims and their ability to rise above their instincts and fears.

Many conflicts of the twentieth century were eventually resolved with compromises that did not include mass repatriation of refugees. Such was the case, for example, with the Sudeten Germans, and in the German-Polish conflict over the German refugees from the German territories, which were annexed to Poland in 1945. These former enemies understood that the return of millions of refugees was actually liable to destabilize the new reality. They preferred to dampen the pain of the past for the sake of an opportunity for the future.

If we accept the "right of return" principle, hundreds of thousands—perhaps millions—of Palestinians will move into a country which they have for years sworn to destroy. Before long they will become the largest population group here. Yet their principal aspiration has been to fight Israel and its symbols, and it is this heritage that they have passed on to their children. Is there a country in the world that can agree, of its own free will, to take in such a population? Can Israel, whose civil society is fragile already, do so without falling apart?

Furthermore, even if the Jews continue to remain a majority in Israel for another ten or twenty years, they will not be a majority for long. When they do become a minority, my fear is that they will be tempted—just like any nation that senses that its hold on its own country is slipping out of its hands—to establish an apartheid regime based on military might or on prejudicial and draconian legislation. This would inevitably lead to an explosion and the collapse of the country's political framework.

If, on the other hand, an Arab majority rules and legislates in Israel, it will be able—by the most democratic of means—to eradicate the state's Jewish character, to rescind its status as a land of refuge for the Jews of the world, and thus merge it with its sister Palestinian state. And is it possible to eliminate completely the ever-present threat of Arab propaganda from outside Israel, according to which every Jew who was not born in this country, or whose parents were not born here, will be forced to return to their country of origin?

I'm sorry, but no thanks. I don't want to be part of a Jewish minority in Israel. This, keep in mind, is the only country in the world that was established by decision of the United Nations, so that the Jewish people would no longer suffer from the anomaly of being a stateless minority dependent on the mercy of others. And I can only agree with Professor Edward Said, who responded quite honestly in a recent interview in the Israeli newspaper *Ha'aretz* to the question of whether a Jewish minority in a Palestinian state would be equally and fairly treated. "It worries me a great deal. The question of what is going to be the fate of the Jews is very difficult for me. I really don't know. It worries me."

I believe with all my heart that the Israelis and the Palestinians can maintain good neighborly relations and heal the wounds that they have inflicted on one another in the past. But I also know, soberly and painfully, that this requires much time. If we can gradually heal the wounds of our wars, we will be able, in the future, to reach a situation in which, perhaps, national definitions will soften a bit and even borders will be no more than a formal line on a map. Perhaps then Israelis and Palestinians, who are much like each other in their natures and passions and, I also believe, pragmatism, will be able to mingle with each other naturally and normally. When that time comes, they will be able to live among each other, in Israel and Palestine, and serve as models of coexistence. In the meantime, we must make do with repairing what can be repaired, healing what can be healed, and trying to achieve a partial justice for both sides rather than absolute justice for either. Then we can finally set out on a new life for all.

## Hours Before the Elections

FEBRUARY 2001

*Prime Minister Barak resigned from office on December 9, 2000, following a long struggle to maintain his coalition government. His pro-peace position was weakened by a growing support for the right-wing parties that called for exercising greater military force in repressing the Intifada. Ariel Sharon, leader of the Likud Party and a former general as well, promised voters in his campaign both peace and security. After months of terrorist attacks and dozens of Israeli victims, this is what the Israeli public was yearning for. Israel was about to vote for a new prime minister. There was no doubt as to the outcome of these elections.*

Today I ran into a reservist who served with me in the Lebanon War. Children were born to both of us back then. He sighed as we spoke. In 1982 Ariel Sharon led us into a trap in Lebanon. How awful it is to think that the children born to us then are the soldiers that he will lead tomorrow, should he win.

There you have it, the whole story: Sharon remains; only the soldiers change.

Sharon's misconduct in that war led a national commission of inquiry to disqualify him from ever serving as Minister of Defense. In any properly run country he would have left public life and shut himself up at home. But in the Israeli political system one of the surest ways to success is to collect a large number of failures (and that will, apparently, be Ehud Barak's only hope after tomorrow).

A non-Israeli may have trouble understanding the secret of Sharon's seduction of the Israeli public. But the average Israeli perceives Sharon as a "strong man" who has spent his entire life fighting the Arabs and has had the courage to face them down. Over a period of more than fifty years, Sharon has had a part in every important military and political campaign, and in many respects he is, for Israelis, one of the last living Sabra heroes, the native-born Israeli who is daring, rooted in the land, and prepared to fight for it to the death. In both his appearance and character he reminds many of a biblical figure—a man of great physical prowess and primal urges, cunning, shrewd, and brave.

On the other side stands Barak. Until he became prime minister, he was considered Israel's most courageous soldier. But now he is considered a man who lost his determination and nerve, groveling before the Palestinians, agreeing to all their demands. To most Israelis, Barak has been willing, in exchange for a tenuous chance at achieving an ambiguous peace, to abandon Judaism's most sacred sites and Israel's strategic assets.

Sharon's plan is astonishing in its simplemindedness and illogic. He declares that he will not evacuate even the tiniest settlement in the territories. He announces that, as far as he is concerned, "compromise" means a willingness not to reoccupy the territories that have already been handed over to the Palestinian Authority. Yet, on top of all this, he promises Israel a "secure peace." Apparently most Israelis long to believe him, and will most likely vote for him.

On second thought, this is no surprise, as Palestinians are murdering Israeli civilians almost daily. The average Israeli, who knows nothing about Palestinian suffering or losses, is certain that the Palestinians are only squeezing more and more concessions out of Israel, with their ultimate goal being not compromise but the destruction of Israel.

So when Sharon comes along and promises that he's got a solution, the despairing Israeli prefers to believe him rather than to come to terms with the fact that the present path, the frustrating path of negotiation, with its painful compromises, is the only path we have that can lead to peace.

Sharon is selling Israelis a miracle cure—he says he won't negotiate under fire. "If they shoot, we don't talk." To put it in simple language, Sharon is prepared to place the future of the peace process, Israel's future, the future of the entire region, in the hands of every fifteen-year-old boy from Nablus or the Deheisheh refugee camp who's got a Molotov cocktail hidden behind his back. Because if they shoot, we don't talk.

Sharon promises, with absolute certainty, to "wipe out terrorism." Despite his decades of run-ins with terror, he has still not learned that it can't be obliterated by military means alone. One can certainly not wipe out the struggle of a nation with a solid national consciousness, motivation, and both great hope and great despair.

Do any of Sharon's supporters really believe that he will have any more room for maneuver than Barak has had? Can anyone today seriously believe that Israel will always be able to do whatever it pleases in the Middle East, without paying a terrible price for it? Will Israel always enjoy American support for realizing its belligerent fantasies? Will there eternally be enough Israelis to follow their leaders into more wars that could have been prevented?

This writer has much criticism to level against Ehud Barak. Against the way he acted, his style of interpersonal relations, his tactlessness toward both those close to him and his enemies. But I am certain of one thing: it would have been impossible to lay one's hand directly on the deepest part of the Israeli-Palestinian wound—as Barak did—without causing an eruption of the kind that has occurred. It couldn't have been done without awakening all the most primal fears, instincts, insults, and loathing, without shaking the cratons on which the two peoples, the Israeli and the Palestinian, live.

I do not see today any other leader who would have dared to put the very core of this historic conflict on the table, raising all the most underlying questions about the Israeli and Palestinians identities, boundaries, and true existential concerns.

Barak did it. Not with great enthusiasm, certainly, not with profound personal recognition of the need to concede and compromise. Most of all, not with respect for his Palestinian partner, or with real sensitivity for his suffering and his plight. But, little by little, by twists and turns, we saw him shake off the illusion of force, the adamant and narrow military view of the world.

Do we now have no choice but to wait for Sharon to change as well? To wait for him to recognize the limits of force, the limits of reality, and reach the same insights that Barak did? What price will we all have to pay for Sharon's schooling? And who can promise us that this man will transform himself, his way of life, his character, to their very roots?

Israel's citizens have never before faced a decision that demands such responsibility and maturity, such a need to overcome their fears. The Israeli public must act against the wild instinct to vote from the gut, to punish the Palestinians, the left, Barak, and reality itself, which demands such difficult and threatening compromises from them. But those who are not prepared to delude themselves, who live here in this tormented and turbulent region, know deep inside that there is no choice but to carry on with this difficult and frustrating process—to continue, while making concessions, to manage this complex conflict with wisdom and resolution, until finally, slowly, some years from now, the conflict fades away.

In a few hours we will know—not only who Israel's new prime minister is, but also to what fate we have condemned ourselves and the entire Middle East.

# After the Elections

FEBRUARY 2001

*Ariel Sharon won an unprecedented landslide victory over Ehud Barak. Barak announced in his concession speech that he was resigning from the Knesset and party leadership. Later he rejected an offer to be appointed Minister of Defense. Sharon proceeded to create a unity coalition government that included members from the defeated Labor Party, the right, and the centrist and religious parties. The resulting cabinet government was the largest in Israel's history, with twenty-eight ministers. The unity government was dismantled in October 2002, when Labor ministers resigned over the national budget debate.*

When Ariel Sharon made his victory speech on Tuesday night, his supporters whistled in contempt and loathing each time their leader mentioned Barak, the left, and the Palestinians. The Israeli public has clearly punished that triad in the most painful possible way. As one voter said, in naïve sincerity, "I'm not sure that Sharon is the best for Israel, but the Palestinians deserve him!"

May I register my suspicion that Ariel Sharon himself does not believe what has happened to him? This man, whom many had already eulogized as a has-been, this power-obsessed, devious extremist of questionable behavior who has failed in nearly every public office he has held, who has ruined nearly everyone who has been his ally, has now been handed an entire country. He can experiment on it with his views and his impulses. Unlike in the past, this time there is hardly anyone who can stop him. But perhaps that is precisely the reason that in the final days of his campaign, when his victory was already assured, Sharon's mood suddenly changed.

Sharon, who has a cynical and venomous sense of humor, and an almost compulsive urge to crack jokes, looked melancholy and lifeless during the days leading up to the election. One of his associates was quoted saying, "It's as if something in him turned off." At moments, perhaps for the first time in his life, he looked almost frightened.

All his life Sharon has operated from the position of the oppositionist, even when he was a cabinet minister. He always, but always, challenged the authority of his superiors, both in the military and in parliament and government. A large part of his military and political careers was based on circumventing authority, disobeying orders, inciting against his leaders, and even—as in the case of the Lebanon War—deceiving his superiors.

And now, suddenly, at the age of seventy-three, he himself is the supreme command. He is authority. He is the man who is responsible for the country.

And there is no one to stop him.

Now he is prime minister of one of the most complicated countries in the world, deep in the most delicate situation it has seen for decades. Perhaps Sharon knows, deep in his heart, that if he does indeed mean to ensure his country's future, he will have to abdicate many of the opinions and beliefs and symbols that he has valued for the past generation. If he refuses to do so, there can be no doubt that he will lead Israel into a full frontal collision, not only with the Palestinians, but with the entire Arab world.

Perhaps that's why Sharon is worried. Paradoxically, this anxiety, and this initial awareness of his true political responsibility—and of the complexity of the dilemmas that only a leader is forced to face—are encouraging signs that we can take comfort in today (since there is no other hope).

In this context it is interesting to note that, when the right has come to power, there has always been a sense that its leaders do not feel truly confident at the wheel. Something in the rhetoric of Israel's right-wing prime ministers, from Begin to Netanyahu, has continued to be opposition rhetoric, dissent against some lawful regime, even when they themselves were the regime. There were periods during Netanyahu's term, for example, when the government itself behaved as if it were a minority group being persecuted by some wraithlike hostile administration, as if it did not really believe in its own legitimacy.

If such will be the situation again, we will soon witness a dangerous eruption of Israeli policy. This is liable to be expressed in more aggressive behavior on the outside, along with contemptuous arrogance toward our neighbors. (Remember, Sharon instigated the Lebanon War in order to allow the Palestinians to take over Jordan!) This will also ignite the atmosphere within Israel and make its social and political polarization more severe. The experience of the years when the right ruled warns us of spectacular acts, which more often than not take place on the boundary between the grotesque and the catastrophic.

The most extreme, fanatic, and fundamentalist groups are now returning to the center of Israel's public stage. The hopes of the moderate, liberal, secular center to turn Israel into a truly democratic country, less militant in character, more civilian in nature, more egalitarian, have been dealt a resounding blow.

Again, there is that old, disheartening feeling that due to an unfortunate series of events, and because of our historical trauma, Israelis are doomed to repeatedly make the same old mistakes. To once again accelerate settlement in the occupied territories and escalate the conflict between our neighbors and us. Once again, the rule that applies to our private lives has come true: over and over again we stumble precisely in those places where we are most in need of redemption, of being reborn.

Immediately after he was elected—as during his entire campaign—Sharon invited the Labor Party to join a national unity government. There can be no doubt that in this he expressed the wishes of many Israelis on both the right and the left who yearn to re-create the sense of partnership and kinship that are so lacking in Israel today. It is difficult, however, to understand what policies the two parties can unite around. Yet if they do succeed in finding a middle ground, Israel will find itself prisoner of that same familiar tragic error that it has been trapped in for years. Once again Israel will present the Arab world with a position that is a respectable compromise between its center-right and center-left blocks. But this compromise will have almost no relation to the demands and anguish and hopes of the Palestinians—that is, no connection to reality. Israel will again conduct virtual negotiations within itself, between itself and its own fears. Then it will be astonished, and perhaps even feel betrayed, when the Palestinians throw its offers back in its face and instigate a new Intifada.

As for the Palestinians, when they declare that as far as they are concerned there is no difference between Sharon and

Barak, they know full well how significant the difference is and what the outcome will be. This might be the reason why the Palestinians hurried, in the two weeks leading up to the Israeli elections, toward a compromise with Israel at the Taba talks. It is unfortunate that this zeal was not evident in the preceding weeks or months. It is also unfortunate that Arafat did not succeed in taking control of his people. He could have channeled the authentic energy of the early Intifada into reaching an agreement while Barak was still in power. Palestinian terrorists murdered dozens of innocent Israelis, women and children among them, during the election campaign. Each funeral, each orphan's tears, supposedly proved to the Israeli public that Barak had erred in agreeing to compromises. The public was practically pushed into the arms of the man who promised them he would not negotiate under fire. The despair and anxiety that possessed Israelis—and their total lack of awareness of Palestinian pain and suffering—are the reasons for Sharon's rise to power.

What is obvious from these elections is that the Israeli public is not yet ready for peace. Israelis crave peace, of course, but they are not yet able to pay the heavy price that such an agreement requires. As for the Palestinians, they too, apparently, have not yet internalized the need for the painful compromises that peace requires. It is impossible to predict how we can get out of this impasse without another round of bloodshed.

Fairness requires that we give Sharon a chance to prove that he is right. But there is a heavy, glum feeling in my heart. It is one thing to report about a train running off the tracks from a vantage point to the side. It is entirely another experience to report it from inside the train.

# Death as a Way of Life

MAY 2001

The horrible thing that's happening to Israelis is that they're getting used to it. They're used to waking up in the morning and hearing about the terrorist attack that occurred at dawn. They're used to the sight of their injured and dead. Used to the stock phrases about the situation, to the formulaic photographs and news. They've gotten so used to it that their emotions sometimes also seem like clichés. Like something that could be put into a compact, blaring newspaper headline in one of the tabloids: ANGUISH AND ANGER! or FEAR AND LOATHING!

There seems to be no way out, to the point that a person doesn't dare, sometimes, to feel anything more than what the headlines proclaim. He dreads that introspection might reveal emotions even more disconcerting and menacing. He dreads that these feelings will kindle disquieting questions about the justice of his actions, or his chances of living, even for a single day, a life of serenity, a life in which he will cause injustice to no one and will fear no Other.

Most Israelis now believe that the peace process has dissolved and become part of history. Even worse, most of them now believe that it was a mirage from the very beginning. They even have trouble understanding how they allowed themselves to be led on by the left and by the Barak government, which deluded them into believing that Israel really had a negotiating partner and that the Palestinians had really given up their dream of destroying Israel.

Israel has plunged into a kind of apathy. Seemingly, life goes on as usual. Everyday affairs are conducted with the characteristic Israeli mixture of vigor and edginess. But as anyone who has lived here all his life knows, everything has a strange and disheartening kind of impassivity. Life in slow motion. Israel is now slipping back into the psychological stance that is most dangerous for itself—the stance of the victim, of the persecuted Jew. Almost every threat to it—even from the Palestinians, who can never defeat Israel on the battlefield—is perceived as an absolute peril justifying the harshest response.

Unlike at other, similar difficult periods in the past, it appears as if Israelis no longer have any hope. Only hope can impel them to try to extricate themselves from this fatal ossification. The prophecy is liable to fulfill itself. "You can't make peace with the Arabs" is a statement I hear very often, every time I foolishly get into a debate on the street, in a taxi, or on a radio program. With one small difference, it is the same statement one hears in debates with Palestinians: "You can't make peace with the Israelis."

The war is taking place almost everywhere in Israel (at this very moment, as I write, I can hear the rumble of the Israeli incursion into Palestinian Beit Jala, six miles due south of my home in a Jerusalem suburb). Despite this, the average Israeli seems to be able to repress what is happening around him and, in a strange way, is almost able to ignore it. It's hardly surprising—decades of wars and anxiety have trained him to do this very efficiently. When an Israeli citizen opens his eyes in the morning, he can assume, with a high degree of certainty, that during the course of the day at least one Israeli will be hurt in an attack of some sort. He knows that his life could change in the bitterest possible way. He won't think about it. Nor will he think about what the Palestinians are feeling (it's all their fault anyway, the average Israeli believes—we offered them everything and they responded with lynching and terrorism). He won't go to crowded places. He'll refrain from hiking his favorite trails, avoid taking roads previously attacked. He contracts himself a little, but no more. He notes that downtowns look empty and bleak. That there are almost no tourists in the streets, and sometimes more policemen and soldiers than civilians. He gets used to that, too. In the evening, in front of the TV news, after the segment on the day's funerals in Tel Aviv and Gaza, a little voice in his head whispers, "Fortunately it wasn't me today."

Gradually, Israelis and Palestinians are moving further away from peace. Just three months ago, in February 2001, at the talks in Taba, an agreement was imminent. Today that looks like a remission, brief and delusional, in the course of an incurable disease. Now almost no one uses the word "peace." The Palestinians say they won't end their violence "until the occupation is completely over." Israel declares that it will not even enter negotiations "until violence comes to a complete halt." Each side knows that its ultimatum—even if morally correct—is unrealistic. Furthermore, both know that if they adhere to these demands they will be caught in continuous violence and that finally they will bring destruction on themselves. The occupation will go on, and the violence will not end (quite the opposite!). In any case, with a kind of numbing of the senses, they do nothing to save themselves from this nightmare.

Since there is no hope, Israelis and Palestinians go back to doing what they do—shedding the blood of each other. Each day more people join the ranks of the dead and wounded, of the haters and the despondent. Each day the appetite for revenge grows. The Palestinians say, before camera and microphone, that they no longer care if there is never an agreement. "The main thing is for the Israelis to suffer as we have suffered." Israelis demand that Prime Minister Sharon "rub out a few Palestinian villages" and believe, so it seems, that this will make the Palestinians surrender and agree to an Israeli compromise.

Senior Palestinian officials, who in private conversations with Israelis severely criticize Arafat and the blind slaughter committed by suicide bombers, close ranks with the most extreme elements in their society when they speak in public. The voice of Israel's left wing has gone almost completely mute—many have given up and have decamped to the right, while others realize that their views just don't resonate with the public at large. Indeed, what influence can ideas and words have in the face of the brutal, all-pervasive reality that eats away at hope like acid?

Instead of pursuing what Arafat likes to call "the peace of the brave," both sides are busy keeping a bloody, you-killed-me-I'll-kill-you balance sheet. The principal objective is to avenge yesterday's murder while minimizing the enemy's retaliation tomorrow. Without noticing it, Palestinians and Israelis are reverting to the pattern of an ancient tribal vendetta, eye for eye and tooth for tooth.

It makes one suspect that the two peoples *prefer* to preoccupy themselves with this cruel ritual rather than really solve the problem at its roots. On second thought, it's easy to understand (especially for anyone who lives here). "They give birth astride of a grave," Samuel Beckett wrote in *Waiting for Godot*, and in the Middle East this description is terribly concrete: all of us, Israelis and Palestinians, were born into this conflict, and our identity is formulated, to no small extent, in terms of hostility and fear, survival and death. Sometimes it seems as if Israelis and Palestinians have no clear identities without the conflict, without the "enemy," whose existence is necessary, perhaps critical, to their sense of self and community.

You become queasy these days listening to that unique form of self-directed *Schadenfreude* that fills Israeli and Palestinian leaders when their angry prophecies come true, in particular as a result of their own failings. They especially like to watch hope collapsing before their eyes. No less shocking is the enthusiasm with which so many Israelis and Palestinians adopt these despairing visions. When it comes down to it, so it seems, people get used to the injustices history has inflicted upon them, to the point that they forget what they are allowed to yearn for.

Sharon and Arafat are both cynical leaders. Their consciousnesses were shaped in war and violence, and their actions mirror each other like a carefully choreographed ceremonial dance. In order to achieve a compromise, both will have to renounce most of the fundamental concepts that have molded their worldviews and that have given them their standing among their peoples. Their actions in recent months make one suspect that they are deliberately making negotiations conditional on demands that have no chance of being met today. They direct government and society, including the media (which in the Palestinian Authority is mobilized to achieve the regime's goals, and is also significantly mobilized in Israel as well), in order to divert the citizenry's attention from the main issues and to manipulatively fuel hostility toward the people of the other side.

As things look now, only a miracle or catastrophe will change the situation. If you don't believe in the first and fear the latter, you realize that the only practical hope for saving Israel and the Palestinians from mutual slaughter is heavy international pressure on both of them. I still believe that Israel has the obligation to make the larger concessions in negotiations, because it is stronger, and because it is the occupier. But *both sides* must immediately end their uncompromising rhetoric and reduce their violent actions to the bare minimum, in order to resume negotiations. Another, more minute hope is for the willingness of individuals, Israelis and Palestinians, to renew open dialogue among them. This is not easy to do, but if such contacts take place, they will be of great and not merely symbolic importance. They will remind both nations of what they must long for. They will create the only alternative to hatred and despair.

## International Intervention, Please

JUNE 2001

*On June 1, 2001, after a particularly bloody period of constant terrorist attacks on Israelis inside Israel and in the West Bank and Gaza, a suicide bomber detonated himself in the middle of a large crowd of young Israelis outside a discotheque on the Tel Aviv beach. Most of the victims were Russian emigrants, many of them teenage girls. Under immense international pressure and a cry for restraint on both sides, Arafat publicly condemned the attack and promised to control his militias. The Israeli government threatened that if there was not an immediate end to terror, harsher military measures would be taken against the Palestinians.*

Twenty-one boys and girls were murdered yesterday in a suicide attack committed by a Palestinian at a discotheque in Tel Aviv. Dozens more were seriously injured. Boys and girls of fourteen or slightly older. Two of them were sisters. None of them was a soldier. They bore no arms. They were children who had come to a birthday party.

This time the bomb was especially evil—besides the explosives, it contained hundreds of heavy ball bearings. Their effect on a human body is terrifying. Yesterday, when the attack was reported in the media, Palestinians went out into the streets of their cities and fired their rifles in the air to celebrate. Even in terms of the cruel dosages of violence that we have become accustomed to in recent years, this attack crossed a boundary. The international community seems to be beginning to comprehend the depth of the hatred and despair among both peoples, and their inability to free themselves from the trap they have so foolishly entered.

It seems to me that it is difficult today to argue against Israel's right to defend itself by retaliating against the Palestinian Authority. There is no government in the world that would hold itself back after the incessant cruel and deadly attacks in the last ten days. And yet, with all due understanding of the anger and urge for revenge that have seized the Israeli people, we need to say: *Force will not resolve the severe crisis between Israel and the Palestinian Authority.*

The two sides have been drawing each other's blood for almost one hundred years. Tens of thousands have already lost their lives. Yet the Arabs have not succeeded in destroying Israel, and Israel has not succeeded in cementing its occupation by force. These truths apply today as well, perhaps even more pointedly than before: perhaps the conflict between Israel and the Palestinians will have no political solution, either, without intense pressure from the international community. The two sides simply are not able today to return to a psychological state in which they can begin a movement toward compromise and conciliation. The darkest days of the Jewish-Arab conflict have not seen such polarized positions, so saturated with hatred and suspicion, as we see today.

It may well be that Arafat has lost control of his people. That is a frightening possibility, and recent events require us to discuss it seriously. I'd submit that even if it is true, no one ought to be too pleased about it, definitely not the Israelis. A crumbling Palestinian Authority, fired up because of what it sees as the "achievements" of terror—especially a Palestinian Authority that has surrendered to Hamas and Islamic Jihad—may bring a horrible catastrophe on itself, on Israel, and on the entire region.

Still, it may well be that Arafat did not order his men to prevent the recent terrorist attacks because he knew he would not be obeyed. If this hypothesis is true, it means that his declaration of a cease-fire this morning has no validity—just like dozens of his similar announcements in the past.

Arafat is now paying the price of flirting with terror. In recent years he has, time after time, released from his prisons Hamas terrorists who have committed attacks against Israel. He has done so to pressure Israel. For years he has been riding on the tiger's back—that's the local expression—and now the tiger has thrown him off and confronts him.

Of course, Israel cannot be absolved of responsibility for Arafat's weakened position. For years Israel has done everything—even during the negotiations after the Oslo Accords—to strengthen its grip on the occupied territories. The Palestinians watched as Arafat was forced to make ever-greater concessions, while the Israeli settlements grew before their eyes and many Israeli roads were paved through the territory promised to the Palestinians. It is clear that this has strengthened the position of the extremists, at the expense of Arafat and of peace.

Here is the essence of the tragedy: two peoples whose extended struggle has distorted their ability to act in a measured way and save themselves from themselves. Today, with eyes wide open—but perhaps blinded by hatred and fear—they are marching toward a terrifying confrontation.

The only thing that can prevent this horrible fate is swift international intervention. A summit should immediately be convened in the region itself, an emergency conference of the European Union's heads of government, the UN Secretary-General, the leaders of those Arab countries that have an interest in putting out this fire, and a senior representative of the President of the United States. Afterward, international forces should be sent to the region to create an impermeable barrier between Israel and Palestine. Concurrently, negotiations should be imposed on the two sides, based on the understandings reached at Taba five months ago. This is apparently the only way that they will make the painful compromises that they are unable to make on their own. All those who see themselves as friends of Israel or of the Palestinians cannot stand aside, at a time when the two peoples are preparing for what may be the beginning of a long war.

## Time to Part Company

AUGUST 2001

*A mother, a father, and three of their children were among the fifteen killed in the suicide bombing of the Sbarro pizzeria in downtown West Jerusalem. Another 130 people were injured, including many more children on their summer vacation. The terrorist responsible for planning this attack appeared on a most-wanted list of terrorists previously submitted to the Palestinian Authority by Israel. Arafat condemned the attack, but failed to take concrete steps to prevent further killings.*

Jerusalem's main street was built more than a century ago, and it's engaging in its simplicity and shabbiness. It's lined with two rows of antiquated, outdated stone construction plastered with huge billboards. The X-shaped crosswalk painted in the middle of the central intersection is the city's heart. There is no child in Jerusalem who does not know it, and for many it is one of the quotidian symbols of civilian Jerusalem—if you've crossed the street there, if you've gotten intermingled, as everyone does, in the flow of people coming at you, you've felt as local as a native.

A Palestinian terrorist picked that X as a target. He chose a vacation day, one on which many of the families sightseeing in Jerusalem stop in at one of the inexpensive downtown restaurants. As I write this, there are already fifteen dead, among them entire families and many children. There are also more than a hundred wounded. When I saw the footage of the crosswalk on television after the attack, my first thought was: This is hell, and I'm living in it.

I turn on the television and hear Palestinian spokesmen explaining with great fluency why the terrorist did what he did. Yasir Arafat will, apparently, issue an official condemnation of the attack. But who will that condemnation help so long as Arafat refuses to arrest those whose intentions to commit such attacks are known to all? At this hour the Israeli cabinet is convening to discuss how to retaliate. Tonight or tomorrow it will come, the response. But will it really change anything? Will it be of any use to the dead? It won't even be of any use to the living.

For more than ten months now, the two sides have been in a mad, dizzy spiral of violence. They don't know how to stop. In the lunatic logic of this conflict it is possible, of course, to justify every murder by citing the murder that preceded it. The cruel code of the Middle East states that if you have not responded with full force to the blow you suffered, the other side will interpret it as weakness and will strike at you again even more painfully. The result is that each side is condemned to strike out at its antagonist, and then cringe in anticipation of the counterblow. The rhythm of life, the rhythm of consciousness, even contacts between one person and another, everything is conducted entirely according to the tick of this deadly metronome. In such an atmosphere, who even remembers that the real goal that we must aspire to is not the next attack on the enemy, or effective protection against him, but to attempt to bring this cycle of death to an end? We suffer so much from the outer, violent symptoms of the situation, and we are so focused in our treatment of them—of them alone. So much so that we have entirely forgotten that only if we are cured of the disease itself, at the source, will we cease, perhaps, to suffer from its symptoms.

The Palestinian Authority is shattered and disintegrating. Palestinians are hungry and hopeless. When the doors are closed and the windows shut, they are vociferously critical of the way Arafat is conducting their affairs. They are also quickly awakening from the illusion that the world—and the United States in particular—will rush to their aid. Israelis are no less desperate. They cannot understand the reality in which they have been living for the last ten months. They are afraid to leave their homes, and especially, they despair at the thought that they will have to live this way for many years to come.

Israel has vast military power—but it cannot use it out of fear that it will lead to international intervention and the imposition of a solution not to its liking. The Palestinians are weak, and yet they are able to cause Israel great pain. Is there a third way? Of course there is: the painful separation of the two peoples, forming two separate sovereign states, Israel and Palestine. To this end, intensive and determined negotiations must be commenced at once. And don't wait, not for a halt to terror, or for mitigation of the siege of the Palestinian population (neither of these will happen, regrettably, in the near future).

Are the Israelis and Palestinians capable of this? The answer, I'm afraid, can be found in Thomas Mann's story "Mario and the Magician": "Between not willing a certain thing and not willing at all . . . there may lie too small a space for the idea of freedom to squeeze into." And, indeed, after more than a century of saying no to each other—in every way possible—it seems as if Israel and the Palestinians are not capable today of wanting *anything* at all. Not even the right thing for themselves, the thing that will promise them life. As for freedom of some sort, freedom of choice, of desire, of hope—it is almost impossible to talk about that anymore.

## Terror's Long Shadow

SEPTEMBER 2001

*This article was written a week after the terrorist attacks of September 11, 2001.*

A dark shadow has fallen over the citizens of the United States and Europe. As an Israeli who has lived his entire life in fear of terrorist attacks, I can say quite simply: Terror embitters life. It imposes a "military" mode of behavior on a person, places him in a constant state of stress.

This slowly percolates throughout one's life and pollutes it. The terrorists don't have to make too much of an effort—from the moment they inject fear into the hearts of citizens, from the moment they persuade the populace that they have no limits, they can make do with sporadic attacks. Fear will soon spread like a flesh-eating bacterium.

The combat aircraft now flying over New York are only the beginning. Gradually, Americans and Europeans will find themselves surrounded by an endless number of security systems. Meant to defend people, these systems actually make them more anxious and less secure. Countless policemen and security guards and SWAT teams and uniformed and plainclothes detectives will be deployed at the entrances to cinemas, theaters, and malls. Guards will check visitors to schools and preschools. But are there enough guards to oversee everyone who goes down into the subway? How many hours before the football game will people have to be at the stadium so that the guards can search the bags of each and every fan?

In Israel, if you lose your handbag, or if you leave your suitcase unattended for a minute to go buy a bus ticket, upon your return you're likely to find it being detonated by a sapper robot. Many streets are closed off in Jerusalem each day because of suspicious objects. All Israelis know that they must allow double the normal time to get anywhere because of these security controls. Boarding an El Al plane is a complicated matter, involving interrogations and personal searches. It's almost like trying to get into a prestigious college.

A large segment of the workforce holds security-related jobs. Huge amounts of energy, invention, and creativity that could have gone into science or technology and into improving the quality of life are channeled into security. Personal freedoms and rights are restricted and taken away in order to protect life. You can be sure that at this very moment every Western state is installing a dense web of surveillance over private telephone calls and E-mail traffic. Thousands of innocent civilians are being arrested, and will continue to be arrested, in an effort to prevent the next attack. An entire army of secret agents will now be allowed to invade every private, intimate area.

In the years to come we will see more people carrying firearms in the streets of the United States and Europe. This massive presence will affect every little run-in and confrontation, even over parking spaces. The violence and murder rates will rise. People will be lighter on the trigger. "I thought he was a terrorist" is an acceptable justification for shooting people in terror-stricken areas.

It's not only countries that will be trapped by the security networks they use to protect "normal life" (except that life long ago stopped being normal). This coarse, stiff coating will also cover the individual soul, the soul of each human being. That is the immediate result of living in fear, in suspicion of every unfamiliar person. It is the way every normal person defends himself against the pain of what is liable to be taken from him at any moment. It is the inability to believe in normality even for a minute. Every habitual sequence of events is but an illusion, and he who is tempted to believe in it will not be prepared for the blow when it comes. Maybe that's the worst thing of all—the person who lives for a time in the shadow of terror no longer knows how enslaved he has become to the struggle for survival, and how much he is, in fact, already a victim.

It is painful to admit, but in a certain sense terror always succeeds. The war against it, and the process of becoming accustomed to what it does with our lives, slowly perverts all that is precious and human, all that makes life worthwhile.

The frightened civilian very quickly composes his own internal mechanism that identifies and catalogues strangers by their racial/national/ethnic traits. Like it or not, he becomes more of a bigot, more susceptible to stereotypes and preconceptions. It is not hard to predict that, under such conditions, the political parties that feed off xenophobia and racism will flourish. Nor is it hard to predict how bitter the lives of minorities will be, especially those who, in outward appearance, match the profiles of the suspect terrorists.

Just a few weeks of life in the shadow of the fear of terror will show every nation that believes itself enlightened just how rapidly and sharply it can turn needs into values, permit fear to determine its norms. Terror humiliates. It rapidly sends a human being back to a precultural, violent, chaotic existence. It determines where society's breaking point is. It entices certain groups, not small ones, to join it, and to actively seek to use force to destroy and crush everything they hate. Terror contains something that acts like a digestive enzyme—it decomposes the private human body and the body politic.

Terror also sharpens one's awareness that a democratic, tranquil way of life requires a great deal of goodwill, the true goodwill of a country's citizens. That is the amazing secret of democratic rule, and also its Achilles' heel. All of us are, when it comes down to it, each other's hostages. Terrorists act on this potential, and so unstring the entire fabric of life.

I regret having to write so bluntly. This is unbearable for me, too, because as I write, I myself realize how great the price is that I, as an Israeli, pay each and every day and moment, in each and every dream at night, in each and every morning farewell to my children.

But it is now, when we are still overcome with shock, when every sane person is in despair over the evil and cruelty of which people are capable, that I want to reiterate something. We, all of us, have so much to lose. That which is most precious to us is so fragile. Countries that fight terror fight not only for the physical security of their citizens. They fight also for their humanity, and for everything that makes them civilized.

# Seven Days: A Diary

OCTOBER 2001

*This article was commissioned by the French newspaper* Libération *as part of a series of personal diaries by authors.*

**SATURDAY, OCTOBER 13, 2001**

Saturday's a great day to get your bomb shelter in order. As my wife and I do our best to clear out all the junk that's piled up there since the last time we thought there'd be a war (it wasn't that long ago, just a year back, when the Intifada broke out), my young daughter is busy making up the list of friends she wants to invite to her upcoming birthday party. A weighty question: Should she invite Tali, who didn't invite her to *her* birthday party? We discuss the problem, trying to mobilize all the gravity it deserves, just so that we can at least keep up an appearance of routine. But the terrorist attacks in the United States have in fact robbed us of that illusion, of the possibility of depending on some sort of logical continuity. A thought is always hovering in the air: Who knows where we will be a month from now?

We already know that our lives will not be as they were before September 11. When the World Trade Center towers collapsed, a deep, long crack appeared in the old reality. The muffled roar of everything that might burst out can be heard through the crack—violence, cruelty, fanaticism, and madness. The wish that we might keep what we have, keep up a daily routine, suddenly seems exposed and vulnerable. The effort to maintain some sort of routine now seems so touching, even heroic—to keep family, home, friends together.

We decide to invite Tali.

**SUNDAY**

I'm lucky that the suggestion to write this journal came as I was beginning to write a new story. If it weren't for that, I'm afraid my diary would have been quite melancholy.

Several months have gone by since I finished my last book, and I felt that not writing was having a bad effect on me. When I'm not writing, I have a feeling that I don't really understand anything. That everything that happens to me, all events and statements and encounters, exist only side by side, without any real contact between them. But the minute I begin writing a new story, everything suddenly becomes intertwined into a single cord; every event feeds into and imbues all other events with life. Every sight I see, every person I meet is a hint that's been sent to me, waiting for me to decipher it.

I'm writing a story about a man and a woman. That is, it began as a short story about a man alone, but the woman he met, who was supposed to be just a chance passerby who listens to his story, suddenly interests me no less than he does. I wonder if it is correct, from a literary point of view, to get so involved with her. She changes the center of gravity I had planned for the story. She disrupts the delicate balance it requires. Last night I woke up thinking that I ought to take her out entirely and replace her with a different character, someone paler, who wouldn't overshadow my protagonist. But in the morning, when I saw her in writing, I just couldn't part with her. At least not before I got to know her a little better. I wrote her all day.

It's almost midnight. When I write a story, I try to go to sleep with one unfinished idea, an idea I haven't gotten to the bottom of. The hope is that at night, in my dreams, it will ripen. It is so exhilarating and rejuvenating to have a story help extricate me from the dispassion that life in this disaster zone dooms me to. It's so good to feel alive again.

### MONDAY

I keep reading hostile remarks about Israel in the European press, even accusations that Israel is responsible for the world's current plight. It infuriates me to see how eagerly some people use Israel as a scapegoat. As if Israel is the one, simple, almost exclusive reason that justifies the terrorism and hate now targeted against the West. It's also astounding that Israel was not invited to participate in the anti-terrorism coalition, while Syria and Iran (Syria and Iran!) were.

I feel that these and other events (the Durban conference and its treatment of Israel; anti-Israeli Islamic incitement and racism) are causing a profound realignment in Israelis' perceptions of themselves. Most Israelis believed that they'd somehow broken free of the tragedy of Jewish fate. Now they feel that that tragedy is once again encompassing them. They're suddenly aware of how far they still are from the promised land, how widespread stereotypical attitudes about "the Jew" still are, and how common anti-Semitism is, hiding all too often behind a screen of (supposedly legitimate) extremist anti-Israel sentiments.

I'm highly critical of Israel's behavior, but in recent weeks I've felt that the international media's hostility to it has not been fed solely by the actions of the Sharon government. A person feels such things deeply, under the skin. I feel them with a kind of shiver that runs back to my most primeval memories, to the times when the Jew was not perceived as a human being of flesh and blood but was rather always a symbol of the Other. A parable, or a chilling metaphor. Last night I heard the host of a BBC program end his interview with an Arab spokesman with the following remark (I'm quoting from memory): "So you say that Israel is the cause of all the troubles that are poisoning the world today. Thank you, and I'd like to wish our audience good night."

**TUESDAY**

For two weeks already there has been a decline of sorts in the level of violence between Israel and the Palestinians. The heart, so accustomed to disappointments, still refuses to be tempted into optimism, but the calm allows me to get absorbed in writing without pangs of conscience. The woman in my story is becoming more of a presence. I haven't the slightest idea where she is leading me. There's something bitter and unbounded about her that frightens and attracts me. There's always that great expectation at the beginning of every story—that the story will surprise me. More than that, I want it to actually *betray* me. To drag me by the hair, absolutely against my will, into the places that are most dangerous and most frightening for me. I want it to destabilize and dissolve all the comfortable defenses of my life. It must deconstruct me, my relations with my children, my wife, and my parents; with my country, with the society I live in, with my language.

It's no wonder that it is so hard to get into a new story. My soul is on guard. Like every living thing, it seeks to continue in its movement, in its routine. Why should it take part in this process of self-destruction? What's wrong with the way it is? Maybe that's why it takes me a long time to write a novel. As if in the first months I have to remove layer after layer of cataract from my recalcitrant soul.

**WEDNESDAY**

"The only one smiling is the one who hasn't heard the latest news." So wrote Bertolt Brecht. At 7:30 in the morning the radio reports the assassination of Israeli Minister of Tourism Rehavam Ze'evi. Ze'evi was an extremist who advocated transferring the Palestinians out of the West Bank and Gaza Strip. I never agreed with his opinions, but such an act of terrorism is horrible and unjustified. That is also my opinion when Israel murders a Palestinian political figure.

Like every other country, Israel has the right to defend itself when a terrorist bearing a "ticking bomb" is on his way to attack. Rehavam Ze'evi, despite his views, was not a terrorist.

The heart fills with apprehension. Who knows how the situation will deteriorate now? Over the last two days there was relative calm, and we were almost bold enough to resume breathing with both lungs. Now, all at once, it's as if the trap has closed in on us once again. I am reminded of how easily we can be overcome by the unbearable lightness of death (as I write, have the feeling that I am documenting the last days before a great catastrophe).

Still, last night I had a small, private moment of comfort. As on every Tuesday, I studied with my *hevruta.* It's two friends, a man and a woman, with whom I study Talmud, Bible, and also Kafka and Agnon. The *hevruta* is an ancient Jewish institution. It's a way of studying together and sharpening the intellect through debate and disputation. During our years of study together, we have developed a kind of private language of associations and memories. I'm the nonreligious one of the three, but I've already had ten years of vibrant, exciting, and stormy dialogue with these soulmates. When we study, I become intimately connected to the millennia-long chain of Jewish thinkers and creators. I reach down into the foundations of the Hebrew language and Jewish thought. I suddenly understand the code hidden in the deep structure of Israel's social and political behavior today. In the midst of confusion and the loss that surrounds me, I unexpectedly feel I belong.

**THURSDAY**

Things fall apart. Israeli forces are entering the Palestinian city of Ramallah. A day of combat. Six Palestinians are killed, a ten-year-old girl among them. Another of the victims was a senior official of Fatah, the majority Palestinian faction, who was responsible for the murder of several Israelis. An Israeli citizen was killed by Palestinian gunfire coming from the village of another, previously killed, Fatah operative. The fragile cease-fire is no more, and who knows how long it will take to rehabilitate it. I call one of the people I can share my gloom with at such a moment. Ahmed Harb, a Palestinian writer from Ramallah, a friend. He tells me about the shooting he hears. He also tells of the optimism that prevailed among the Palestinians until the day before yesterday, before Ze'evi's murder. "Look how the extremists on both sides are working hand in hand," he says. "And look how successful they are . . ." Only two days ago Israel lifted its siege of Ramallah for the first time in weeks. After Ze'evi's assassination the roadblocks returned. I ask him if there's something I can do to help him, and he laughs. "We just want to *move*. To be in motion. To be able to leave the city and come back . . ."

Between the news bulletins, amid the ambulance sirens and the helicopters that relentlessly circle above, I try to isolate myself. I battle to write my story. Not as a way of turning my back on reality—reality is here, in any case, like acid that eats away any protective coating—but rather out of a sense that, in the current situation, the very act of writing becomes an act of protest. An act of self-definition within a situation that literally threatens to obliterate me. When I write, or imagine, or create even one new phrase, it is as if I have succeeded in overcoming, for a brief time, the arbitrariness and tyranny of circumstance. For a moment, *I am not a victim.*

## FRIDAY

The week is coming to an end. Its events were so acute that I did not have time to write about many important things dear to me: about my son, who is writing a surrealist play for his high school drama club; about the soccer game we watched together on television, Manchester United *vs.* Deportivo la Coruña (with Barthez's outrageous blunders); about my daughter, who is conducting a scientific study of her parakeet; about my eldest son, who is serving in the army and about whom I am anxious each and every moment. Also, about our twenty-fifth wedding anniversary this week, celebrated this time with much concern: Will we succeed in preserving this vulnerable family structure in the years to come?

So many cherished things and private moments are lost to fear and violence. So much creative power, so much imagination and thought, are directed today at destruction and death (or at guarding against destruction and death). Sometimes there is a sense that most of our energy is invested in defending the boundaries of our existence. And too little energy is left for living life itself.

## Deadly Routine

DECEMBER 2001

*On November 29, 2001, four Israelis died in a suicide attack on a bus near Hadera, north of Tel Aviv. On December 1, twelve people were killed and 180 wounded in a downtown Jerusalem attack carried out by two suicide bombers and a car bomb that exploded twenty minutes later, timed to strike the oncoming rescue teams. On December 2, a suicide bomber blew up a crowded bus in Haifa, killing fifteen and wounding over forty more. Another bus was destroyed in the attack. On December 5, a suicide bomber blew himself up near a bus stop in the center of Jerusalem. Eleven people were wounded. On December 9, Israeli policemen at a busy junction north of Haifa shot a suspicious-looking terrorist. The explosives in his belt detonated, wounding thirty-one people.*

One p.m. These are the moments of fear after the terrorist attack in Haifa. The radio speaks of as many as fourteen dead and about fifty wounded from the explosion of a suicide bomber in a bus. They're all civilians.

Each ring of the telephone might be announcing terrible news from relatives and friends who live there. One young cousin isn't answering her cell phone. We know that she had been planning a ride on bus number 17, the route on which the attack occurred.

My finger desperately punches the numbers of the hospitals to which the victims were evacuated. Has she been admitted? The operator at the emergency center looks down the list. Seconds that last forever. We think about her. Of what it will be like without her.

The radio broadcasts recordings of cheers from Hamas's radio station in Nablus. "We will avenge your death, O Abu Hanud," they promise the Hamas official murdered by Israel last week, after he had murdered dozens of Israelis. The operator gets back to me: No, sir, the name you gave me is not on our list. We can breathe again.

But we really can't breathe. Incidents run into one another. Another shooting here, another alert about a suicide bomber there. Between the reports, the announcements of the funeral times for the ten young people killed the previous night as they sat at a café in Jerusalem. It is terrifying how one event blacks out the previous one. It was only yesterday, after midnight, that we anxiously telephoned all our friends and the parents of our children's friends who were out at that hour at the place where the attacks occurred. "Lucky that there's a big history exam today," my son explains to me lucidly. "That's why most of my friends stayed home to study last night."

The giddy madness. The Hamas terrorist's mother ululates joyously—her son will now enter paradise. She's only sorry that he died this way—that is, "because he was killed without taking twenty Israelis with him." After the shooting attack in Afula last week, someone, perhaps unintentionally, covered the body of an Israeli woman who'd been murdered there with an old election poster proclaiming ONLY SHARON WILL KEEP US SECURE. And, in fact, this same Sharon declared three days ago, "We have found the way to deal with the security problem."

We have already seen the first Israeli retaliation—attacks on Arafat's headquarters and helicopters. But I'm sure that what we have witnessed is only the beginning of Israel's response. When Sharon spoke today, there were war drums in his voice. He promised an escalation in Israeli retaliation operations. But who remembers that each escalation by Israel brings about an escalation of terror in turn?

From the way Sharon is talking, it's clear that the unthinkable is now quiet thinkable—toppling the Palestinian Authority, expelling Arafat; all now seems possible. Only one alternative isn't being considered at all: immediately commencing intensive negotiations, without preconditions.

On the other side, Arafat. This is the Arafat who, when notified by Israel that there is a sophisticated explosives factory in Nablus, confiscates the explosives and immediately releases the terrorists. Arafat, who speaks ceaselessly about his opposition to terror but who refuses, out of cowardice and shortsightedness, to finally instigate a courageous battle against the terrorist elements in the Palestinian Authority. He doesn't understand that it is they who will bring an end to his great dream, and perhaps to himself, too.

How can we bring to a halt this madness in which we are becoming blind, becoming filled with anxiety and despair, forgetting that on the other side there are, at this moment, people like us, anxious and despairing? In other words, how can we make Arafat talk less and do more, and how can we bring Israel to do less and talk more?

In the days to come, Israel will apparently launch a massive military offensive. The Palestinians will respond with even more terrorist attacks. It's amazing how the Israelis and Palestinians never turn off this path, the path of violence. The bungled Oslo Accords are, for most Israelis and Palestinians, resounding proof that they can never again walk the path of peace.

It is now 3 p.m. I note the hour because there's no way of knowing what will happen after I send this article off. I have already written so many articles at moments like these, after attacks, before attacks. I've tried so many times to understand, to explain, and to find the logic behind the actions of both sides. What I feel like doing now is not writing an article. I actually feel like taking a can of black spray paint and covering every wall in Jerusalem, Gaza, and Ramallah with graffiti: LUNATICS, STOP KILLING AND START TALKING!

## Turning a Blind Eye

DECEMBER 2001

*The U.S. Middle East envoy, General Anthony Zinni, left the region on December 16, 2001, after failed attempts to broker a cease-fire between Israel and the Palestinians. During Zinni's three weeks in Israel, over a hundred Israelis and Palestinians were killed in a resurgence of hostilities. An earlier shooting attack by Palestinian terrorists on an Israeli bus in the West Bank settlement of Emmanuel, which killed ten and wounded dozens, provoked Israeli air strikes in retaliation. Sharon announced that the Israeli government was breaking off all ties with Yasir Arafat, who was at the time under personal siege by the Israeli Army in his headquarters in Ramallah.*

Six months ago the journal *Nature* published a study about a dangerous mechanism in the human visual system. The study sought to explain why the brain sometimes refuses to see what the eyes take in and convey to it. The scientists, from Israel's Weizmann Institute of Science, suggested that the explanation for this phenomenon is that the brain is flooded with a multitude of interpretations of every reality it faces and that it must, in the end, decide in favor of one of them and act accordingly. The fascinating part of this explanation is the hypothesis that, from the moment the brain decides in favor of a given interpretation of the images it is receiving from the eyes, all stimuli that support any other interpretation simply disappear. The brain, as it were, refuses to incorporate them.

In the impossible relationship between Israel and the Palestinians, both sides have for years suffered from almost complete blindness to the complexity of the situation. Each is certain that the other side is ceaselessly deceiving it; that the other side does not want peace at all; that any compromising move by the other side is camouflage for an intrigue designed to bring that side victory and the elimination of its opponent.

Despite all that, early this week, at an army roadblock near Ramallah, several dozen of us, peace activists from both sides, gathered. In the middle of the chaos of hundreds of backed-up and churning vehicles, of people trying uselessly to leave or enter their city, in the face of the shouting and cursing of Palestinians who oppose this desperate initiative to bring people together, Yossi Beilin, one of the fathers of the Oslo agreement, and Yasir Abd Rabbo, the Palestinian Minister of Information and Culture and a close associate of Yasir Arafat, called for a swift resumption of dialogue. Or at least acceptance of American envoy Anthony Zinni's proposal for a forty-eight-hour cease-fire.

The rest is well known. Neither side honored the cease-fire. Many Israelis and Palestinians did not survive even these mere forty-eight hours. Wednesday night, after an especially bloody attack by Hamas, the Israeli government issued an odd and equivocal statement: Arafat was *irrelevant*; he was blotted out of the picture. This meant, actually, that the Palestinian people had also been blotted out, along with their justified desires and aspirations. And so any tiny chance for talks, for an agreement, for a more tolerable future, was also blotted out.

A person stands before this reality and his heart breaks in

seeing how the fears and suspicions and worldviews of naysayers succeed, in the end, in proving themselves in the most destructive possible way. How endless malicious, mistaken acts by each side have connected one link to the next in an ostensibly logical continuum—logical in the distorted terms of the conflict—until, all at once, it becomes clear how we have ourselves, with our bare hands, garroted our own necks with a bloody chain of violence.

And it could have been otherwise. One can sketch a picture of more merciful circumstances. One's thoughts skip quickly back. Had Jordan's King Hussein responded to Moshe Dayan's invitation to call him, immediately after the 1967 War, to discuss peace between the two countries; had Israel initiated, in talks it held with the Palestinians in the 1970s and 1980s, a bold settlement that would have linked Israel, Jordan, and Palestine in a federation; had Sharon, when he was Minister of Defense in 1982, not tried to evict Arafat from Lebanon to Tunis but rather had allowed him to return to the occupied territories as a leader; had Israel addressed the first Intifada, in 1987, as a Palestinian cry of distress, and tried to respond accordingly rather than simply to repress it; had Yitzhak Rabin not been assassinated; had Hamas suicide bombers not killed hundreds of Israelis in Jerusalem and Tel Aviv in 1995 and 1996, thus helping Benjamin Netanyahu win the prime ministership; had Ehud Barak negotiated at Camp David with greater wisdom and sensitivity; had Arafat had the good judgment to realize the magnitude of the Israeli concessions on offer and not turned so quickly onto the path of violence in September 2000; had Sharon not gone to the Temple Mount; had Arafat truly fought terrorism and not tried to fool the whole world; had . . .

As the list grows longer, a bitter feeling wells up that perhaps there really was no other way. That the two nations still are not ready for peace. That neither of them even comprehends what peace means. That even if they know, in theory, how to talk about the "need for peace," they do not have the strength to go through the profound and painful processes required to bring it about and make it successful. A small number, much too small a number, are still capable of the mental and emotional effort that the complexity of the situation requires. Within the dread that I sense around me, at times I hear a sigh: "Let it end already, one way or another, even in war, but things simply cannot go on as they are now!"

This morning, in the face of the events coming one on the heels of the other, there is no escaping this conclusion: The Israeli brain and the Palestinian brain, which have never known a single day of real peace, have been conditioned to perceive one unambiguous picture of reality—that of the unending war, of the one-dimensional, stereotypical, monolithically hateful, violent enemy.

Yet, even now, even more than at any other time, we cannot allow ourselves to give up the idea of peace. Attempts at peace, even if they sometimes seem, as I know they do, pathetic, even virtual, are of significant importance in preserving some link between those Israelis and Palestinians who agree that there is no solution other than a political solution. But we must recognize, with much grief, that at this point, there is no chance for a political settlement between the two sides. I don't think I have to explain what that implies.

# QED

JANUARY 2002

*On January 3, 2002, the Israeli Navy intercepted the* Karine A, *a ship heading for the Palestinian Authority's port at Gaza with a cargo of 50 tons of arms and ammunition. Israel claimed that the Palestinian Authority, Iran, and Hezbollah had collaborated in this smuggling operation.*

The capture of the Palestinian arms ship means we can breathe easier. This profusion of weapons won't be aimed at Israel. There's also a sense of gratitude toward the soldiers who participated in the raid. But the voices of the spokesmen for the army, the government, and the media evinced an undisguised joy at having finally found "conclusive evidence" of the Palestinians' nefarious terrorist intentions. As they would have it, it is now beyond a doubt that "the Palestinian Authority is infected with terror from the soles of its feet to its scalp," as Shaul Mofaz, the army's chief of staff, declared at the press conference. He seemed to be trying, for a moment, to bring back the glory of the heroic 1950s, or even of the legendary Entebbe operation of 1974.

But what proof is this? It is proof that if you oppress a nation for thirty-five years, humiliate its leader, abuse its people and offer them no hope, that nation will seek to protect itself however it can. Would any of us act differently than the Palestinians if we faced the same situation? Didn't we, in fact, do exactly the same during the years we spent, at different times in our history, under occupation and tyranny?

Avshalom Feinberg and Yosef Lishansky traveled to Cairo in 1916 to get money for the Nili underground organization so that the Jewish community in Palestine could defend itself against the Turks; members of the three underground organizations of the 1930s and 1940s—Haganah, Lehi, and Etzel—acquired and stashed away as many weapons as possible, and the caches where they hid these arms still symbolize the Jewish struggle for survival and freedom. We still admire the Zionist fighters who participated in daring operations to capture arms during the period of the British Mandate, operations that the British considered acts of terror.

But when *we* performed such exploits, they were not terrorism. They were the legitimate actions of a nation that was fighting for its independence. When the Palestinians behave similarly, it is seen as proof of everything that we have been so keen to prove for years.

It was embarrassing and infuriating to hear Mofaz and the Minister of Defense, Benjamin Ben-Eliezer, lecture to the Palestinians about how they are "wasting their money on arms instead of taking care of their hungry, indigent population." These are the words of men whose soldiers—following instructions from the government—are abusing Palestinians day and night, depriving them of food and property. It was no less distressing to observe the Israeli press coverage of the ship's capture. The reporters, awestruck at the heroism of our soldiers, without exception embraced the sanctimonious assertions of the prime minister and the chief of staff, who claim that murder and terrorism burn in the hearts of Palestinians almost as second nature.

Now we'll have the celebrations, the glee of "we told you so": We told you that the Palestinians don't keep agreements (unlike us, of course, who honor all agreements). We told you that they will do anything to obtain offensive weapons (whereas we only aim daffodils at Arafat's window in Ramallah). We told you that there's no one to talk to, so we'd better keep tightening the noose around their necks (that way we'll definitely bring about a profound change in Palestinian nature, so that they'll agree to conditions). We told you that Arafat is, in fact, bin Laden himself (yet we are all disciples of the Dalai Lama).

In their attempt to smuggle the ship in, the Palestinians grossly violated their agreements, and the Israeli Army must, of course, do all it can to thwart such escalation. Nevertheless, how can we dull the judgment of an entire nation? How can we keep ignoring the big picture, the acute feeling that Israel—in its deeds and its blunders, and especially with the malicious behavior of its prime minister—is pushing the Palestinians further toward such actions, which provide us, time and again, with that "conclusive evidence"—evidence that is of absolutely no real use to us in achieving our goals?

These are repulsive times. Times in which good sense has been reduced to a zombie-like stupor. Prime Minister Ariel Sharon will squeeze every last drop of propaganda out of this ship. The media, for the most part, will fall in line behind him. The Israeli public, too tired and apathetic to think, will accept every categorical statement that will supposedly resolve the difficult internal contradiction and moral dilemma it is living with and will reinforce its shaken sense of its own justice. Who today has the strength to recall the beginning, the root of the matter, the circumstances, the fact that this is about occupation and oppression, about retaliation and counterretaliation, about a vicious cycle of blood, about two peoples who are turning corrupt and violent, and finally insane?

## Hail, Caesar!

FEBRUARY 2002

*In the weeks preceding this article, the sides continued their escalation of the fighting. Despite American efforts to mediate, the talks for a cease-fire and for renewed negotiations reached an impasse. The article was written after a press conference in which Ariel Sharon vowed to fight terrorism by all means necessary.*

Carry on, Caesar. Death awaits us everywhere, but carry on. Our inconsequential lives, our inconsequential deaths, should not trouble you. You have a plan. We are thus certain that all we see each day is but a prelude to something more successful, to a brilliant concept that will, in an instant, change the scenery. Know this, Caesar: we only appear to be without hope. We only appear to feel like dead men walking. Soon, in a month or two, you will come before us to present the idea that will guarantee us full security. Peace with security. We are secure in your peace, Caesar. We feel it approaching with long, brisk strides. You will compel our enemies to love us no matter how much we oppress them. You will rid yourself of their ruler and put another, deferential and obedient, in his place. Then their hearts will, in the blink of an eye, come to love us, resign themselves to our mistreatment of them, and even declare it just.

But, Caesar, we beseech you, could you please be a little quicker about it? We are not complaining, heaven forfend. Nor do we have any doubts about your ability to reinvent human nature. It is plain to us that you are the man who can finally redesign our enemies so that they will resign themselves to whatever you offer them, even with your absolute refusal to offer them anything at all. The fact that no nation, however powerful, has yet succeeded in maintaining a conquest of this type, in these conditions, is no law of nature. We will be the first! Why not? Just, we beseech you, be quick about it, because soon—how can we put it?—no one will remain, neither soldiers nor civilians.

Times are a bit hard, Caesar—you may have noticed. Of course you have noticed, but you are strong, stronger than we; this is beyond doubt. We are weak of mind and faint of heart, and there is nothing to be done about it. That is why we need you. You must lead us with all the force at your disposal, with the help of our army, which is among the strongest armies in the world, toward a new future. Perhaps we'll call it the Retaliation Era, in memory of your bold cross-border revenge operations against Palestinian guerrillas in the 1950s, when the lives of Palestinian women and children were no obstacle to your military objectives. In that future, each attack by Palestinian guerrillas will bring on a counter-attack from us. They will strike at us here, and we will strike at them there; they will blow up people in our streets and we will bomb their homes. It's inspired! A perfect and effective use of our might!

True, sometimes a slight doubt, a stray, worthless thought steals into our hearts. Ludicrous thoughts about different definitions of courage and cowardice, of certainty and surrender. Sometimes a false demon insinuates in our ears that perhaps the most horrible surrender of all is our slow, vegetative submersion into oblivion and apathy, without any attempt to save ourselves. Sometimes an evil tongue wags seditiously that even with the bad hand of cards we were dealt—despair, Palestinian carnage in our cities, the settlements, that impossible Arafat—it would have been possible, somehow, to play a better game. To take advantage of every opportunity for mitigation and compromise, to be smart and not just right. To use a bold, generous, farsighted political initiative to create a new situation. But against this towers the decisive, unchallengeable claim: We've already tried it! We already offered everything and they refused and betrayed us! We will never repeat that fatal mistake. We will always face forward, toward those methods and tactics and operations that have been so successful in the past, that have brought us to where we are. So, Caesar, continue to fight to the last drop of our blood, so long as you continue to draw blood from our enemies as well. As one we vow, like Samson, to die with the Palestinians. They deserve it.

Though sometimes, we confess, we are a bit confused. Forgive us for this. Nevertheless, when we hear what some of your cabinet ministers say, about ever-harsher military responses, about reconquering the Palestinian territories, about deporting four million Palestinians, and so on and so forth, a fundamental, simple bewilderment steals into our hearts. Is your program really so cunning and sophisticated that it also has an answer to the new circumstances we will create if we carry out such ideas? Or perhaps, for the purpose of attaining your goals, you have made a strategic decision to move the battlefield not, as military strategy mandates, into enemy territory, but actually into an entirely different plane of reality, into an entirely absurd multidimensional space, into absolute self-annihilation, where neither we nor they will exist. There will be nothing. Nothing will be.

But, of course, all these thoughts are of no consequence. Your loyal citizens have no doubt as to your wisdom and vision. Very soon, clearly, all will realize that there was a profound and hidden reason why we were compelled to live this way for so many years, in contradiction of all logic. It is the reason why we consented, as if we were at the theater, to suspend our disbelief until, at the denouement, all is comprehended. And for this same obscure reason we also pledged to subvert the underpinnings of our democracy, of our economy, of our security itself, and of the possibility that we will ever have a tolerable future here.

Either way, when these reasons and motives, currently concealed from us, are finally revealed, we will certainly understand why we were sentenced to live here for decades on the sidetrack of the life that was meant for us, and why we consented to live our own irreproducible lives in a kind of latent death. Until then, we will continue to support you wholeheartedly, and even as we go to die, in the tens, hundreds, and thousands, we salute you, Caesar.

## Reality Check, March 2002

APRIL 2002

*Following the most grisly terrorist attack since the Intifada began, on Passover evening at the Park Hotel in Netanya—in a month of daily terrorist attacks that killed over eighty civilians—the Israeli Army invaded Ramallah and other cities in the West Bank on March 27, 2002. Despite international condemnation, the operation received widespread support, as a terrorized Israel rallied behind the army and government. Voices and acts of protest were criticized, and opposition to the operation was condemned by many Israelis as treason. Long curfews were imposed on the Palestinian population, freedom of movement almost completely denied. Complaints of violations of human rights reached the world and Israel, despite the army's frequent refusal to allow access to journalists and aid workers. Most major Israeli media complied with the restrictions. The Israelis were accused by the Palestinians of committing a massacre in the city of Jenin, but international reports later confirmed Israel's denial. Nevertheless, an Amnesty International report published in November 2002 condemned the Israeli government and army for committing war crimes against civilians.*

Seven days ago, as Israel was celebrating Passover, one of the Jewish people's most significant holidays, more than a score of Israelis were murdered by a Palestinian suicide bomber who planted himself in the center of the hall where they were seated around their holiday tables. Survivors relate that the man took a long, slow look around, examining their faces, and then calmly detonated himself.

In response to this, and to three other deadly attacks that happened soon afterward, the Israeli government ordered its army to mobilize twenty thousand reservists and to launch a large-scale campaign against the Palestinian Authority known as Operation Defensive Shield. Today, Israeli tanks are surrounding Yasir Arafat's compound in Ramallah in an act that lacks any political rationale. Suddenly one bullet, accidental or deliberate, can change the face of the Middle East and catapult all of us into war. Every day, meanwhile, Palestinians are exploding in the streets of Israel, killing dozens.

There is not an Israeli who does not feel that his life is in danger, and the despondency and dread that this insecurity causes are again exposing the odd paradox of Israel's position. On the one hand, militarily and economically it is one of the strongest countries in the Middle East. Its citizens strongly feel that they share a common fate; they are firmly determined to defend their homeland. On the other hand, Israel is also a surprisingly fragile country, profoundly, almost tragically, unsure of itself, of its own ability to survive, of the possibility of a future for itself in this region. These two characteristics are on prominent display right now—Israel is today a clenched fist, but also a hand whose fingers are spread wide in despair.

Excuse my dramatic exaggeration, but I'm writing this from the front lines. Meaning, I'm sitting in the neighborhood café, in the shopping center near my house, in a suburb of Jerusalem. I'm the only customer in the place, which until a few months ago was bustling around the clock. A few shoppers scurry past, their expressions indicating that they would rather be at home. They look from one side to the other, constantly checking their surroundings. Any of the people nearby could be their murderer. That man over there, for example, who has been standing motionless for several seconds at the top of the escalator leading to the second floor. He's putting his hand in his pants pocket now, and I notice that around me other pairs of eyes are watching him nervously. Without even realizing that they are doing it, people step back, toward the walls. What am I supposed to do? What does one do when it happens? What should I be thinking about? The man draws a pack of cigarettes out of his pocket, that's all, just a little colored pack, self-destruction of a normal, comprehensible kind. The film that stopped in freeze-frame for a second continues to roll, until the next scary part.

There is, of course, a clear imbalance of power between the two peoples, Israeli and Palestinian. But there is symmetry in their fear of each other and in their ability to send themselves and their neighbors sliding into an abyss.

Without minimizing Israel's responsibility for the deterioration and without ignoring the immense suffering that Israel has inflicted on the Palestinians during thirty-five years of occupation, I feel today that it is the Palestinians who have brought about the current intolerable escalation. It is the outcome of their choice to use the weapon of suicide bombings against Israeli civilians.

We must recognize this in order to be able to deal with the new situation we are facing. The suicide bombings have injected into an already complex conflict an element that is irrational, insane, inhuman from any perspective, immoral in a way that we have never yet seen, even in this grubby conflict. Suicide bombings are a weapon that no one in the world knows how to confront. Their use, on such a large scale as to make them almost routine, is liable to lead to extremely dangerous Israeli responses.

Today, as the Israeli Army besieges Arafat's office, another terrorist makes his way—of this we can be certain—to an Israeli street, to another bus or shopping mall. At this very hour, as in a scene from a convoluted epic novel, full of reversals, two men face off against each other. These are the leaders of the two nations, Ariel Sharon and Yasir Arafat, two cunning old men, ultimate survivors, and grand masters of a strange game of chess in which they cause the most damage and loss to their own pieces.

Twenty years after Sharon trapped Arafat in Beirut in the Lebanon War of 1982, and after Arafat slipped away to Tunis—striding along the dock at Beirut, on the crosshairs of an Israeli sniper forbidden to shoot him—the two are facing off again.

The sordid reality that the two of them have created for their public is in their own image. Each of them has "succeeded"—each in his own way, each in accordance with the influence he has wielded over the years—in fanning the flames of violence, hatred, and despair among their peoples. Their opponents say that they have no policy and no vision beyond the will to survive. But look how today's situation is the inevitable outcome of their chosen paths, their deeds, their aspirations, and how much the present state of affairs reflects their warlike, suspicious, and aggressive view of the world. For them it confirms, in a hermetic, circular way, just how right they have always been.

Sharon and Arafat have together, in a collaboration that makes the skin crawl, complicated politics to the point that it has turned to war, have spread despondency about any possibility of dialogue, have brought the situation to such an extreme that their people will be seduced into believing that there really is no choice but to fight against and kill each other.

Now each of them plays the role he has perfected over decades. One is the superwarrior, a sort of gigantic military relic of the new Jewish history. The other is the persecuted, isolated, besieged martyr, wallowing in the desolation from which he knows how to draw a startling strength and forcefulness.

Both of them will fail, apparently, just as they have failed in the past. Sharon won't succeed in eradicating terrorism. Even if he captures all its planners and strategists, even if he confiscates all the large quantities of weapons that the Palestinians now possess, he will not succeed in excising from the hearts of the Palestinians the impetus to act violently. That is their despair, their sense of humiliation, and their hatred of Israel. His measures will only enhance all these and encourage further waves of terror that will make Israel's position even more precarious.

Arafat will not, apparently, get what he wants, which is to draw the Arab countries into the conflict. They fear, no less than Israel, the internal unrest that the Israeli-Palestinian conflict causes, and fear even more the Islamic religious extremism that Arafat encourages and that is liable to harm them from within. The world will, apparently, continue to abandon Israel and the Palestinians to kill each other.

More seriously, Arafat's gambits, the encouragement he gives to the suicide bombers, his grotesque hope, as he recently stated, to himself be "a suicide bomber, a martyr, on the way to Jerusalem," only pushes the establishment of a Palestinian state further into the distance.

Evil things are happening to both peoples. Fear causes no less damage to the soul than explosives cause to the body. Israeli society is becoming more violent, aggressive, and racist, and less democratic. Palestinian society is undergoing an even more dangerous process. A society that becomes accustomed to sending its young men and women on suicide operations aimed at murdering innocent civilians, a society that encourages such actions and glorifies their perpetrators, will pay a price in the future. Its coin will be their attitude toward life itself, life as an inalienable sacred value. It will also be paid in a more practical way—the minute the possibility of such a horrifying action is forming in the consciousness of a nation, it will not disappear. It will rear its head again in the people's internal affairs. It is not at all surprising that moderate Palestinians are no less alarmed by the suicide bombers than Israelis are. They know the bitter truth—the weapon of suicide, which has proved itself so effective against the Israelis, is liable to be used against them as well, when the Palestinians have a state and commence their internecine struggles over the character and image of that state.

That's the way things are right now. It's a situation of despair and disintegration. How can we get out of it? Palestinian terrorist attacks will, unfortunately, continue for a long time to come. But if there is also, concurrently, a move toward peace, a process of concessions, of ending the occupation, of conciliation and recognition of the suffering incurred by the other side, there is room for the hope that the Palestinian public's support for terror will decline and the Israeli public's confidence in a peaceful resolution of the conflict will grow. Is there a chance that this might happen? Every thinking person realizes that Arafat and Sharon are incapable of creating this opportunity. What remains? To live through this nightmare to its end, to go from funeral to funeral and to try to survive each passing moment. Thoughts of peace, of mutual understanding, of coexistence between the two peoples now sound like the last signals of life from a ship that has already sunk.

# This War Cannot Be Won

JUNE 2002

*When a bus exploded in the morning rush hour in southern Jerusalem, the sound was heard miles away in other parts of the city. Most of the victims were residents of the neighborhood of Gilo, often targeted by Palestinian snipers. A few of the dead and the wounded were Arab Israeli college students. Arafat made a statement to the Palestinian people the next day, demanding a halt to attacks on Israeli civilians, because such attacks give the Israeli government "the excuse to reoccupy our land."*

Another victory for madness: A moment before President Bush was to make a speech declaring his support for a Palestinian state, a Palestinian suicide-murderer of the Hamas faction blew himself up on a bus in Jerusalem. He killed nineteen civilians and wounded seventy, including children on their way to school. Black plastic body bags were laid out in a row on the sidewalk, one next to the other.

This row of bodies postponed significantly the Palestinians' chances of attaining their own state. Despite this, according to a survey published yesterday in the Palestinian Authority, 80 percent of the Palestinian public supports continued terrorist attacks against Israelis. If that's the case, we must conclude that the Palestinians are now doing everything necessary to ensure that they will never have their own country.

At the same time, the Israeli government is being pushed into a corner. Shackled to its aggressive, mechanical, one-dimensional way of thinking, it immediately declares an escalated response. From now on, the government declares, the Israeli Army will reoccupy areas of the Palestinian Authority following every attack on Israel. Only this time, the army will not withdraw quickly—it "will instead remain in them until terrorism ceases."

Since terrorism won't come to a halt, certainly not as long as there is no political settlement granting the Palestinians an independent state, it is clear that the Israeli government has decided to reconquer the entire area of the Palestinian Authority, in order to ensure that terrorism will continue.

Why is Hamas so eager to harm the interests of the Palestinians as a whole? Because Hamas fears the reforms that Arafat will soon be compelled to institute, reforms that will restrict Hamas's terrorist activities. Hamas is also concerned that the positions of Egypt, Jordan, and Saudi Arabia on the need to fight terrorism are drawing closer to those of the United States and Israel. Hamas's immediate goal is to induce Israel to attack the Palestinian Authority, perhaps even reoccupy its territories, to force these relatively moderate Arab states to retreat into their previous extremist positions.

So why is the Israeli government—under Ariel Sharon's leadership—playing into Hamas's hands?

Because it doesn't believe that it has anyone to negotiate with on the Palestinian side, and because it includes factions that oppose any real compromise. But mostly because the Israeli government is at a loss, confused, and desperate.

Israel is so much at a loss that yesterday a senior cabinet minister proposed that Israel, instead of surrounding itself with a protective wall and fences, surround every Palestinian village and city with fences, to isolate them one from the other.

Israel is so discouraged today that the idea of expelling the Palestinians from the areas of the Palestinian Authority, and expelling Israel's million Palestinian citizens, is gaining support and legitimacy in public opinion and at the cabinet table. Yesterday, at the entrance to Jerusalem, demonstrators who support such a transfer (the euphemistic term for expulsion and deportation) carried this banner: TRANSFER: THE ONLY WAY TO PEACE!

In other words, not dialogue and compromise and mutual recognition and a consensual border and a cessation of terrorism as the way to peace. No, the way to the much-desired peace and tranquillity is to expel a few million more Palestinians!

One gets dizzy listening to such unfounded claims, from seeing the horrors that come hard on the heels of the last, creating a surrealistic continuum in which a madman's logic rules. If we follow each side's line of thinking a little further, we'll easily perceive how we will soon be living—in an endless jumble of murders and expulsions and reoccupations and strategic mega-attacks, perhaps even nuclear terrorism, the destabilization of the moderate Arab states, perhaps even an all-out war whose outcome no one can predict. It feels like a nightmare, and maybe only a historian gazing back from the future will be able to explain the hypnotic effect of the nightmare we are striding into with eyes wide open. Both sides are doing everything in their power, each in its turn, to ensure that it all comes true.

Three weeks ago I went to London to participate in a unique encounter organized by the British newspaper *The Guardian.* Israeli and Palestinian supporters of peace spent three days conferring with the leaders of the formerly warring factions of Northern Ireland. The Irish Catholics and Protestants who had been murdering each other just four years ago sat next to each other and spoke the language of peace, and expressed their grave concern that the conflict might break out again. We, the Israelis and Palestinians, listened to them, with much yearning and envy. At one point, an Israeli asked, How did you do it? How did you manage to extricate yourselves from hundreds of years of violence and hatred and put yourselves on the track of dialogue? When did you understand that there was no other way?

David Ervine, a Protestant leader who had been caught in the past with a live bomb in his hands, looked at Martin McGuinness, a Catholic leader, a man whom he had fought, who had been his bitter enemy. "There was a moment," he said, "when I simply understood that this war cannot be won." McGuinness nodded.

A sigh of relief passed among us, Israelis and Palestinians, relief at having become aware of a conclusion that was so simple, at having heard such a clear, longed-for formulation. But then we grew somber again. We made a quick computation: In Northern Ireland, it took eight hundred years to reach this obvious conclusion. Does that mean that we have another seven hundred years to wait?

(I meant to end the article here. But as I type this, the radio is announcing a warning that a terrorist with an explosive belt is now roaming the streets of Jerusalem. And again the stomach knots up, the thoughts race. You quickly scan your mental map of those dear to you—where is each of them at this particular moment? You visualize a huge roulette wheel, turning slowly, slowly, and then coming to a halt.)

# Bad Fences Make Bad Neighbors

JULY 2002

*Grassroots organizers and politicians from different sides of the political spectrum gained popular support in their campaign for unilateral withdrawal and the construction of a fence separating Israel from the Palestinian Authority's territory. The proposed unilateral disengagement system would include fences, walls, electromagnetic measures, guard towers, airborne surveillance, security patrols, and well-guarded checkpoints. It would not be considered a border. According to its supporters, the fence would serve as a barrier preventing terrorists in the West Bank and Gaza Strip from entering Israel. It would remain in place until a negotiated peace could be achieved with the Palestinians. Yet even among its proponents there was disagreement as to where the fence would run and how many Israeli settlements would be protected on its Israeli side. Ariel Sharon's government finally approved the route of the first seventy or so miles of the fence in August 2002, but stipulated that none of the Israeli settlements outside it would be evacuated.*

*As of December 2002, less than a mile of the fence had been built.*

"Good fences make good neighbors," wrote the poet Robert Frost. Israel and Palestine are certainly not good neighbors, and there is certainly an urgent need, both in practice and in principle, to establish a border between them. I mean a border with sophisticated defensive and barrier devices, open only at border crossings established by mutual consent. Such a border would protect them from each other, would help stabilize their relations and, especially, would require them to internalize, once and for all, the *concept* of a border. It's a vague, elusive, and problematic concept for both of them, since they've lived for the last hundred years without clear boundaries, with constant invasion, each within, on top of, over, and under the other.

Yet, in my opinion, it would be very dangerous to establish such a border fence right now, unilaterally, without a peace agreement of any kind, while the principal points are still in heated dispute, before the two sides have truly exhausted all the possibilities for dialogue between them. The establishment of a fence now, even if it reduces the number of terrorist attacks for a certain period, is another precipitate action aimed at giving the Israeli public a temporary illusion of security. Its main effect would be to supply Israelis with a counterfeit replacement for a peace process that requires difficult and painful compromises.

There may well come a time—after both sides have attempted another serious and sincere move toward peace—when Israel will reach the conclusion that there really is no chance of peace in this generation. In such a case, Israel will have to withdraw from the occupied territories, evacuate almost all the settlements, shut itself behind a thick wall, and prepare for an ongoing battle.

From my conversations with Palestinian leaders, however, I am convinced there still is a chance for peace. And as long as there is a chance, even a slight one, Israel may not make its choice of last resort.

Most Israelis disagree. They think we've already reached that point. "There's no one to make an agreement with!" they say. "Even Shimon Peres and the leaders of the left say that they are no longer willing to talk with Arafat, and in the meantime, Israel must defend itself against terror somehow!"

But even if we assume that Arafat is not a partner (by the way, it certainly hasn't been proven that Sharon is a willing partner either), we need to examine the practical implications of the establishment of a barrier fence without an agreement. They are grave enough to make such a unilateral move unwise, unless there really is no other alternative.

It is clear to everyone that such a fence would not prevent, for example, the Palestinians from firing rockets and mortars from their territory into Israel. If Israel closed itself off behind a fence, the Palestinians would be able to invite in "aid" from foreign armies—from Iran, for example, or Hezbollah. The Israeli Army would have to operate beyond the fence, in order to defend isolated Israeli settlements that remained on the other side. It takes little imagination to realize what military complications this would lead to.

The fence would not provide an appropriate military response to the complex situation in Jerusalem, in which Jews and Arabs live adjacent to one another, rubbing shoulders each day. On the contrary. An attempt to detach East Jerusalem from the rest of the Palestinian territories is liable to turn the Arab city's inhabitants—who, up until now, have seldom been direct participants in acts of terrorism—into active partners in the Palestinian struggle.

People will counter me by asking, What do you propose to do in the meantime, until conditions are ripe for an agreement? Isn't it better to build the fence, so that we can block, at least partially, terrorist attacks?

I wish I could believe that the fence would ward off even some of the attacks in the long run. My fear is that, without a peace process, the attacks it would stop in the short run would simply appear in another, more permeable place. Given the intensity of the conflict, any wall would be a sieve with plenty of gaping holes.

The distress Israelis feel is constant and comprehensible. It derives from the inhuman cruelty of the suicide bombings—the very real threat to one's personal safety—and from the feeling that there is no end in sight, given the huge support for terrorism in the Palestinian public. But this distress cannot overcome the sense that the Israeli infatuation with the fence is the product of a psychological need. It is not a well-considered diplomatic and military policy.

In establishing a fence unilaterally, Israel is, after all, throwing away the major card it has to play. It would be discarding this trump without receiving anything in return from the Palestinians, while the conflict and Palestinian demands and wounds are still at a boil. Yasir Abd Rabbo, the Palestinian Minister of Information, said last month in a conversation with Israelis from the peace camp: "If you withdraw behind the fence, we will spend a day celebrating that most of the occupation has ended, and the next day we will continue the Intifada, in order to obtain the rest of our demands."

Those other demands are well known: Israeli withdrawal from 100 percent of the territories Israel occupied in the Six-Day War; evacuation of *all* the settlements; Arab Jerusalem as the capital of Palestine; and acceptance of the principle of the Palestinian refugees' "right of return" within Israel proper.

Yet there is today a good chance of resolving all these issues in negotiations. The Clinton framework plan, which proposes solutions for all of them, has been accepted, in practice, by both sides, even if neither side is able to commence negotiations to put those solutions into practice. But if these demands are not met and are not resolved in negotiations, the

Palestinians will continue to fight. In fact, they may even fight more fiercely if they feel that their terrorism has forced Israel into a new ghetto. They will, in fact, be rewarded for terrorism and have an incentive to continue it.

Because it is so important, let me say it again: The establishment of a fence without an agreement means that Israel would give up most of the occupied territories without the Palestinians giving up the "right of return."

Furthermore, the establishment of a fence without peace also means that most of the settlements would be included within Israel. But in building the fence in such a way that they are on the Israeli side, Israel would also have to take in a large number of Palestinian towns and villages that lie close to these Israeli settlements and to the roads that lead to them. According to some estimates, this would involve the "annexation" of about 150,000 Palestinians. If we add in the Arabs of East Jerusalem, the number of Palestinians on the Israeli side of the fence may well reach 400,000. These people would not, of course, be Israeli citizens. Israel, after all, does not want them. They would have no clear legal status. Obviously, they would not be able to participate in elections. What, then, would be done with them? How, for example, would Israel pay for their social insurance? (Israel paid for it during its period of military rule, and it cost hundreds of millions of dollars a year.) Does anyone seriously believe that these Palestinians would not become a new incubator for terror of an even more violent and desperate kind? When that happened, they would be *inside* the fence, not outside it, and they would have unobstructed passage to Israel's city centers. Or would Israel confine them behind yet another, second fence? Israel fears the "right of return," because it threatens to return several tens of thousands of Palestinians to within its borders. So it is impossible to understand how Israel could so easily be prepared to take in hundreds of thousands of hostile Palestinians by building a fence.

Another question. Has anyone given thought to how Israel's million Arab citizens would react? Those whose wide-ranging ties with their families in the Palestinian Authority would be severed by the fence? Would Israel not be increasing the bitterness and frustration they feel, and would not this lead them to adopt even more extreme positions (and this at a time when their connection with their country, Israel, has been growing more tenuous)?

So, when we examine the issue, we reach the conclusion that the fence's major drawing power for most Israelis is that, unlike other ideas being floated right now, it is one that has never actually been tried. So it can be believed in, for a while.

The borderline between Israel and Palestine can be set only through full agreement by both sides. Dialogue, as difficult as it may be, has tremendous importance in shaping the nature of the peace to come. Dialogue also contributes to the political maturation of its partners. True, an agreement seems detached from reality today, but even if it is hard to believe in, we cannot allow ourselves the luxury of despairing of it. I think it's even better to wait and live for a few more years without this fence of illusions than to be tempted to build it now. It won't, after all, put an end to terrorism, but only make perpetrators seek other ways to attack, perhaps more vicious ones. Even worse, the unilateral erection of a fence (it would really be better termed a wall) would be a move that would declare our absolute and final despair of reaching a peace agreement in our generation, of integrating a normal Israel into the region around it. In other words, the establishment of the fence may make the conflict permanent and push any possibility of a solution beyond reach.

Too many unilateral moves have been made here. Too many acts of political and military force and coercion. The unilateral establishment of a wall will result in a new and dangerous nadir in this process. A wall would allow the extremists—who are all too numerous—to argue that there would be no one to talk to in the future, either. A wall would allow stereotypes to take root and flourish in the minds of both peoples. Xenophobic and racist thinking would spread even more. Putting the Other out of sight will not solve the problem. It will only make dehumanization easier, and justify a more extreme struggle against that Other.

So, instead of being tempted by dubious ideas like the establishment of a border and the unilateral erection of a wall, it would be better for Israel to invest its energy in the immediate recommencement of negotiations. If Arafat is unacceptable to Sharon and Bush, let those leaders explain to us how they can create a better situation, and how they can assure us—if one could be reassured by such a thing—that Arafat's successor will agree to accept their dictates. Until they can do so, they bear the responsibility, no less weighty than Arafat's responsibility, for the immobility, the insensibility, and the despair on both sides, and for the continued violence and killing.

# Two Years of Intifada

SEPTEMBER 2002

*On the second anniversary of the Intifada, Arafat was under Israeli siege for the second time; terrorist attacks on Israeli civilians inside Israel and in the occupied territories continued, keeping Israeli security forces on constant high alert; the sides were not negotiating a cease-fire; and President Bush was busy building a coalition for an attack on Iraq, planned to take place sometime in the near future.*

I might begin this piece on the second anniversary of the second Intifada precisely two years ago, with the day when Ariel Sharon made his entry into the Temple Mount, on September 28, 2000, and set off a conflagration in the occupied territories. But the story could actually begin in any of the seven years that preceded September 2000. During that period, Israel and the Palestinians did everything in their power to disrupt and confound the delicate agreement they cobbled together at Oslo. Israel doubled the number of its settlers in the territories, and the Palestinians smuggled in weapons, hoarded ammunition, and prepared for war.

Those who were attentive then to the Palestinians' complaints and warnings about the Oslo agreement and the reality it was supposed to make permanent could have seen something was amiss. It offered the Palestinians a tiny state, sliced into segments by a massive Israeli presence. More than anything else, this reality served Israel's stringent security needs. The prescient could have understood then what had to happen.

Few in Israel were capable of listening to the warnings. That is our, the Israelis', historic mistake. The Palestinians themselves joined in the march of folly by responding to Sharon's provocation with an outbreak of unrestrained violence. What happened next is already history, and a tragedy. Two years have gone by. Two years of unlived life for both peoples. Two years of living with our senses, our reason for living, our habits, our hopes dulled and constricted. Two years of gradually congealing thought that could be expressed only in large red headlines.

More than 625 Israelis have been killed in a total of 14,280 incidents in these past two years. Some 1,370 Palestinians have been killed by Israeli military forces. A total of 4,500 Israelis have been injured in terrorist attacks, and among the Palestinians, the numbers are much higher—the Palestinian Red Crescent organization reported two weeks ago a total of 19,649 wounded.

Yet each side is certain that the other side has not suffered sufficiently. That being the case, it's clear that the conflict has yet to exhaust the reservoirs of hatred, and has yet to bring both peoples to the state of exhaustion that will be necessary for them to begin making concessions. Almost the opposite is true—the Palestinians' bloody terrorist attacks have led to a metamorphosis. The thirty-three years of Israel's repression in the territories that it conquered in 1967 (a conquest that was instigated, let's not forget, by the hostile acts of Arab countries against Israel) have nearly been expunged from Israeli consciousness. It's very convenient for most Israelis to believe that now accounts with the Palestinians have been settled, and the blame for the current situation lies entirely on Palestinian shoulders.

And this may well be the root cause of the prevailing despair that any mutual understanding can be achieved. The Palestinians begin their timeline of the conflict from, at the latest, 1948, when the State of Israel was founded. Israelis, for the most part, place the starting point of their timeline at September 2000.

According to this Israeli perception, there is no chance of any compromise now, because "there's no partner," because "the Palestinians are all terrorists," and because "they rejected the generous offer made them by Ehud Barak." The Palestinians also despair in advance of any compromise. In their perception, any agreement that could be achieved now, in the current international climate, would favor Israel, and would certainly not meet even the minimal requirements of the Palestinian people.

In hindsight, the Palestinians' strategic choice to use terrorism as their weapon worked like a boomerang. It severely weakened the moral force of the Palestinian struggle and branded Yasir Arafat as a terrorist in the United States and other parts of the Western World. It also provided a not insignificant justification for Israel's harsh and massive military response. Now, nearly every Palestinian action, even if it is justified resistance to the occupation, is perceived by policymakers in the West as terrorism. To a large extent, this paralyzes the Palestinian cause.

There's an astonishing paradox on the Israeli side. Israel is worse off than it has ever been in the last thirty-five years. Its security, economy, and national morale are in decline. Yet Ariel Sharon, its failure of a prime minister, remains the most popular man in the country. There's a simple explanation. Sharon has succeeded, with no little help from Palestinian terrorism, in getting the Israeli people to restrict their view of their complex conflict with the Palestinians to a single question. Israelis now think solely of their personal security. It's certainly an issue of decisive importance, especially in the current state of affairs. Yet Sharon's political cunning is such that he has succeeded in reducing it to a single dimension, so that the only answer to the great and complicated question "How does Israel make itself secure?" is "By force."

This is Sharon's expertise. Force, more force, and only force. The result is that anytime some small flicker of a chance appears, every time there is a decline in violence, Sharon rushes to carry out another "targeted liquidation" of one or another Palestinian commander, and the fire flares again. Anytime Palestinian representatives declare their willingness to renew negotiations and halt violence and suicide attacks, the response from Sharon's office is dismissal and derision. As far as the current Israeli government is concerned, even if the current Palestinian leadership were to swear fealty to Sharon's Likud Party, the act would be labeled a sinister gambit aimed at gaining legitimacy for the armed struggle against Israel.

Sharon has loyal allies—the extremists among the Palestinians, who are also quick to incite the mob and send endless suicide bombers to Israel's cities each time there seems to be a respite. Each side is thus playing on the fears and despair of the other, each chasing the other around the familiar vicious circle—the more violence increases, the less chance there is of persuading people on either side that there is any possibility of a compromise, pushing the violence up to even higher levels. Day by day the temptation grows to view the opponent as other than human, making any action against him permissible. But those who permit themselves to do anything to their enemies are, for all intents and purposes, declaring that they, too, are inhuman, thus inviting a similar kind of vengeance from their opponents.

So two years have passed. Who has won and who has lost, as of now?

On the surface—and this is true only for this moment—Israel has undoubtedly won. Arafat is losing his international legitimacy. Until just a few days ago, he was losing his hold over his own people as well, as they became ever more aware of his corruption and his failure as a leader. He is now trapped and isolated in the three or four rooms that remain in his headquarters in Ramallah. The senior command level of most of the Palestinian organizations has been killed or captured by Israeli security forces. The people on the second and third command levels are inexperienced in combat, in organizational skills, and in field security. The result is that Israel has been hugely successful in preventing most of the terrorist attacks that the Palestinians have tried to commit.

At the beginning of the Intifada, and especially when suicide attacks increased, it seemed to the Palestinians that Israeli society was weak. They believed, as one Palestinian leader put it, that Israel was no stronger than a spiderweb. Today it is clear that the severity of the attacks and the large number of victims they have claimed have reinforced Israel's sense of national unity and common identity. Israelis today are willing to suffer heavy losses to achieve Sharon's goals.

Yet Israel is paying a high price. Two years into the Intifada, Israel is more militant, nationalist, and racist than it has ever been before. The broad national consensus has placed all criticism and minority opinions outside the bounds of legitimacy. There is almost no significant opposition. The Labor

Party, the shaper of Israel's national ethos in the country's early period, has been digested entirely in the bowels of the right-wing government. Anyone who opposes the brutality of the Sharon government's actions is suspected of disloyalty bordering on treason. The media has, for the most part, aligned itself with the right, with the government, and with the army, and serves as a clarion for the most hawkish and anti-Palestinian line. Sanctimonious self-righteousness, disdain for the "spineless values" of democracy, and calls for the expulsion of Israel's Arab citizens (in addition to the Palestinians in the territories) have become an accepted and legitimate part of the public discourse that no one gets exercised about.

The power of the extremist religious parties is increasing. A wave of crude and sentimental patriotism is sweeping the country. It wells up out of the authentic, historic, and almost primal sensibilities of "Jewish destiny" in its most tragic form. The Israelis, citizens of the strongest military power in the region, are once again, with strange enthusiasm, walling themselves up behind their sense of persecution and victimization. The Palestinian threat—ridiculous in terms of the balance of power but effective in its results—has forced Israel to return, with depressing speed, to the experience of living in fear of total annihilation. This fear, naturally, justifies a brutal response to any threat.

Israel has won, for now, but what is the meaning of victory when it brings no hope for a better future, not even a sense of security and relief? The Palestinians have lost for the moment, but they are now fighting with their backs to the wall, and it is hard to believe that they will surrender and accept Sharon's diktats. It may turn out that, as with the first Intifada, the Palestinians have no stamina for a struggle of more than two years and that, as they did then, they face a period of social disintegration and bitter internal struggle. It would behoove Israel not to rejoice should that happen, because in the end Israel has, or at least should have, an interest in a strong and resilient Palestinian society led by a leadership with a broad base of support. Only such a Palestinian society can sign a stable peace agreement with Israel that will include historic concessions. But such a sophisticated argument cannot today penetrate the dullness of the Israeli spirit and mind. And since Israel is stronger than the Palestinians, the conflict is seemingly doomed to continue as is for an unpredictable length of time.

Two years have gone by and there is no hope. The situation can be summed up in several ways. I choose to do so by citing two facts that stood out in the reports of the last month. The first: According to data provided by UN agencies, more than a quarter of Palestinian children now suffer from malnutrition as a result of the situation. The second: Israeli schoolchildren will soon be given special classes in early identification and detection of suicide bombers. Israelis and Palestinians who refuse to see the connection between these two facts ensure that for many years to come we will all be each other's hostages, agents of gratuitous and pointless death.